CW00815890

Invest Your Humanity

Invest Your Humanity

Celebrating
Marvin Meyer

Edited by
Julye Bidmead
and
Gail J. Stearns

PICKWICK *Publications* · Eugene, Oregon

INVEST YOUR HUMANITY
Celebrating Marvin Meyer

Copyright © 2015 Wipf and Stock Publishers. All rights reserved. Except for brief quotations in critical publications or reviews, no part of this book may be reproduced in any manner without prior written permission from the publisher. Write: Permissions. Wipf and Stock Publishers, 199 W. 8th Ave., Suite 3, Eugene, OR 97401.

Pickwick Publications
An Imprint of Wipf and Stock Publishers
199 W. 8th Ave., Suite 3
Eugene, OR 97401

www.wipfandstock.com

ISBN: 978-1-62564-136-6

Cataloguing-in-Publication data:

Invest your humanity : celebrating Marvin Meyer / edited by Julye Bidmead and Gail J. Stearns ; forewords by Daniela C. Struppa and Elaine Pagels.

xviii + 126 p. ; 23 cm. Includes bibliographical references.

ISBN: 978-1-62564-136-6

1. Meyer, Marvin W. 2. Nag Hammadi. 3. Gnosticism. 4. Schweitzer, Albert, 1875–1965. I. Bidmead, Julye. II. Stearns, Gail J. III. Struppa, Daniela C. IV. Pagels, Elaine. V. Title.

BR50 I60 2016

Manufactured in the U.S.A.   02/19/2016

Cover photo courtesy of Bonita Meyer

This volume is dedicated to Marvin W. Meyer

Marvin Meyer speaking in the Fish Interfaith Center at
Chapman University. Photo courtesy of Chapman University.

Contents

Part 3: Ancient Texts

Foreword

I DECIDED TO JOIN Chapman University approximately ten years ago, and Marv Meyer was one of the reasons that convinced me that Chapman could be a great new home for me.

I was, at the time, a Dean at George Mason University, a large—and research intensive—institution in Northern Virginia. I was intrigued by the prospect of beginning a new phase of my life in beautiful Southern California in an institution that seemed to promise growth, challenge, and excitement. But it certainly was a big step, the one I was going to take. In some way, I wanted to know that my aspiration towards a vibrant intellectual community was something that Chapman would embrace.

This is when I found Marv's name among the faculty of the institution. I immediately recognized the name because of the publicity that had surrounded him for his work on the Gnostic Gospels. While I am just a mathematician, I have always been fascinated by early Christianity and by the spiritual conquests that are hidden in some of the most obscure and lesser known texts of that period.

So, when I came to Chapman, I sought Marv out. In my mind, I expected him to be what the public at large imagines the stereotypical professor of humanities to be: stern, with a deep voice, somewhat haughty, and very cultured. This, at least, is what we see in movies, and we are taught to expect.

Well . . . I got two out of four. Marv had a wonderful booming voice, and he was a man of immense learning. But he could not have been further from stern or haughty. He was a humorous, intensely dedicated, and yet generous man. His intellect, his love for what he did, his interest in learning about others, were immediately evident, and I like to think we became friends the first time we met.

Marv never disappointed me. Throughout the years in which we worked together, he never once lost his sense of humor, his humanity, his love for his students and for his colleagues. I never heard him utter a less than kind word. He was one of those people who practiced—in every day of his life—what he preached. For him, the university was truly what we imagine it should be: a vibrant intellectual community, where ideas are presented, debated, embraced, refuted—always in a spirit of collegiality—and with the certitude that we are all bound by the same unfettered passion for learning and discovering. Students and colleagues become partners in this learning experience and—all together—we transform the community.

I have three specific memories that I want to mention here. The first deals with two friends of mine, two Italian mathematicians that visited me a few years ago. They, as well, knew of Marv Meyer, and wanted to meet him. So we had a wonderful lunch together at the now defunct Lebanese restaurant, Papa Hassan. I remember we discussed the ancient mathematical manuscripts that Marv had seen throughout his career, and we parted with a promise to eventually come back and see whether we could study them together. As it often happens, this collaboration did not develop, but until Marv's passing I had held a hope that we could one day come back together to examine some of those manuscripts.

My second memory is a public one, and one that my colleagues remember well. From the very beginning of my tenure at Chapman, Marv advocated relentlessly for a Faculty Athenaeum, a place where faculty could convene as friends over a glass of wine, and thus develop in a natural way the friendships that lead to mutual intellectual growth. He never stopped pushing for this dream of his, but he always did this with his typical style: never annoying, always supportive. It was one of my greatest pleasures when we were finally able to inaugurate the Athenaeum that we eventually—and appropriately—named after him. The Athenaeum has indeed proven to be a gift to the entire community, and every time I walk through its door, flanked by a beautiful picture of Marv, I am grateful for his commitment and passion for this concept.

And finally, a neverending present. Shortly before his passing, Marv gave me a beautiful autographed copy of his recent translation of The Gospel of St. Thomas. This text is absolutely magnificent, and it opens with a prologue that has since become a part of my own teaching philosophy, and that remains, in my mind, the last teaching that Marv imparted upon me:

> *Those who seek should not stop seeking until they find. When they find, they will be troubled. When they are troubled, they will marvel, and will rule over all.*

Thank you, my friend: we will not stop seeking until we find.

Foreword

Elaine Pagels

WHAT MARV MEYER GAVE us, besides great friendship, were his outstanding contributions as a scholar, shared with a rare generosity of spirit. Marv worked in an extremely challenging field, and gave what seemed to be endless energy to translating notoriously difficult texts and conveying an understanding of them that was subtle, yet accessible to everyone who wished to learn. As his colleagues, we know how exciting it is to work on such scholarly discoveries—and we also know how competitive this can be when the stakes are high. What distinguished Marv was his commitment to collaboration; he never spoke negatively about others, and loved *sharing* the discovery. We all know how his face lit up whenever he met us, the twinkle in his eye showing the deep kindness we always counted on from him.

Although I don't want to startle his family, I can't help mention that Marv was actually my "brother"—or so we agreed on our first trip to Egypt in the 1970s—a time when a woman—especially a westerner—could not walk comfortably in many parts of Egypt unless walking with a family member. So Marv offered to be my "brother" during the days we spent with other scholars living at the sugar factory near Nag Hammadi. During the feast of Ramadan, when digging at the archeological site stopped, Marv, several others, and I took off in an ancient Egyptian taxi to see the Valley of the Kings in Upper Egypt. After hours of marveling at these treasures, we were about to head back for dinner—but there was no bridge there to cross the Nile. Since the taxi driver wanted to keep his customers, he said this was no problem—he'd put the taxi on a raft and take us across. After a dozen men hauled the taxi onto a wooden raft—and us as well—we set off across the river—and slowly realized that the raft was sinking! The driver began to shout that he was losing his taxi because of these crazy foreigners—saying nothing about losing the crazy foreigners—and we were going the way of the Titanic—until a determined band of men with ropes on the other side, cheered on by the whole village, finally hauled the raft up on the other bank. And while I'd been wondering whether to dive and swim—Marv was laughing at what he saw as a grand adventure!

When we were about to head back to Nag Hammadi, police armed with machine guns told us to stop—now the road was riddled with machine gun fire from a blood feud that had broken out ahead. Luckily, one of us had brought a carton of Marlboros and a bottle of Johnnie Walker scotch. After we presented these to the grateful mayor of Luxor, he ordered guards armed with machine guns to escort us on the trip back. I'll never forget—and Marv never let me!—how I dove onto the floor of the taxi at the first hint of action—while Marv "Indiana Jones" Meyer watched with delight, loving every dangerous minute.

Marv brought that spirit of adventure to scholarship too—and shared it with countless students and other people who'd never imagined that there *was* a *Gospel of Thomas*—let alone a *Gospel of Mary* or a *Gospel of Judas*. And he also brought to it his hard-earned knowledge of Greek and Coptic, a keen eye for nuance, and a willingness to wrestle with profoundly difficult texts until meaning emerged. Marv saw being a scholar as a privilege and a responsibility. He was a leader in our field, a collaborator, and in so many different ways, a trusted friend. For many of us, he was indeed much more; he was adventurous, brilliant, generous Marv—our brother.

Acknowledgments

WE WOULD LIKE TO thank our friends and colleagues who share our memories of, and our enthusiasm for offering a volume to celebrate, the extraordinary contributions and person of Marvin Meyer. In particular, we are grateful to Virginia Warren and Marilyn Harran for their support toward the publication of this volume. We thank Daniele Struppa for his contribution as well as for his ever-present encouragement of our work in so many ways. We offer our thanks to Bonnie Meyer for her friendship and care throughout this process. Thanks to each of the contributors of this volume, and to K. C. Hanson with Pickwick for his kind assistance in publication. Special thanks to Marilyn Love for her expert eye in copy editing. Finally, we are grateful for the support of our colleagues at The Fish Interfaith Center and in the Department of Religious Studies at Chapman University.

—Julye Bidmead and Gail J. Stearns

Contributors

Dr. Willis Barnstone is an American poet, memoirist, translator, Hispanist, and comparatist. He was a Guggenheim Fellow and Pulitzer Prize finalist in poetry. He taught in Greece at the end of the Civil War (1949–51), in Buenos Aires during the Dirty War, and during the Cultural Revolution went to China, where he was later a Fulbright Professor of American Literature at Beijing Foreign Studies University (1984–1985). Barnstone is Distinguished Professor at Indiana University. His publications include *The Other Bible* (1984), a memoir biography *With Borges on an Ordinary Evening in Buenos Aires* (1993), and *To Touch the Sky* (1999).

Dr. Julye Bidmead is Director of the Office of Fellowships and Scholars Program and Associate Professor of Religious Studies at Chapman University. She is co-president of the Fish Interfaith Center Advisory Board. Dr. Bidmead received a PhD from Vanderbilt University. She is the author of *The Akitu Festival: Religious Continuity and Royal Legitimation in Mesopotamia* (2004) and numerous articles on ancient Near Eastern religions, ritual studies, and gender. Her current book project, *Recovering Women's Rituals in the Ancient Near East*, explores women's roles in the religions of ancient Israel, Canaan, and Mesopotamia. Dr. Bidmead is Education Director and field archaeologist on the Tel Jezreel Expedition and the Megiddo Expedition in Israel.

Dr. Kathleen E. Corley is the Oshkosh Northwestern Distinguished Professor of Religious Studies at the University of Wisconsin at Oshkosh. She teaches classes in New Testament, Christianity, Gnosticism, and Women in Religion. A member of the Steering Committee of the Women and the Biblical World section of the Society of Biblical Literature, she has also served as Visiting Scholar at the Institute for Antiquity and Christianity in Claremont, California, and the Episcopal Divinity School in Cambridge, Massachusetts. Her books include *How Women Invented Christianity* (forthcoming), *Maranatha: Women's Funerary Rituals and Christian Origins* (2010), *Women and the Historical Jesus: Feminist Myths of Christian Origins* (2002) and *Private Women, Public Meals: Social Conflict in the Synoptic Tradition* (1993).

Dr. Ronald L. Farmer is Adjunct Professor of Religious Studies at Brandman University. Dr. Farmer held the Irvin C. and Edy Chapman Chair as Dean of the Wallace All Faiths Chapel of the Fish Interfaith Center and served as Associate Professor of Religious Studies at Chapman University from August 1997 to January 2011. His books include *Beyond the Impasse: The Promise of a Process Hermeneutic* (1997), *Revelation* (Chalice Commentaries for Today 2005), and *Awakenings* (2009). He was a two-term chair of the Society of Biblical Literature's Bible and Contemporary Theologies Group, served as history consultant for the History Channel documentary, *The Antichrist*, and is the author of over four dozen essays, journal articles, and book chapters. He is an ordained minister in the Christian Church (Disciples of Christ).

Dr. James E. Goehring received a BA in Social Science from the University of California at Berkeley in 1972, a MA in Religious Studies from the University of California at Santa Barbara in 1976, and a PhD from the Claremont Graduate University in 1981. He served as a Research Associate in the Göttingen Academy of Sciences from 1979–81, at which point he assumed the position of an Assistant Director of the Institute for Antiquity and Christianity, and Assistant Professor of the Claremont Graduate University (1981–85). He left Claremont in 1985 to assume his current position as a professor of Religion at the University of Mary Washington in Fredericksburg, Virginia. He has received numerous awards and fellowships, including an Alexander von Humboldt Fellowship (1989–90) and a NEH Fellowship (2002–2003). He has served as resident of the North American Patristics Society (2004–2005), and currently holds a position on the Advisory Board of the *Journal of Early Christian Studies*. His publications in the field of early Egyptian monasticism are numerous. His books include *The Letter of Ammon and Pachomian Monasticism* (1985), *The Crosby-Schøyen Codex: Ms 193 in the Schøyen Collection* (1990), *Ascetics, Society, and the Desert: Studies in Early Egyptian Monasticism* (1999), a co-edited volume titled *The World of Early Egyptian Christianity* (2007), and most recently *Politics, Monasticism, and Miracles in Sixth Century Upper Egypt: A Critical Edition and Translation of the Coptic texts on Abraham of Farshut* (2012).

Dr. Charles T. Hughes is Associate Professor of Philosophy and Religious Studies at Chapman University. He received a Bachelor of Arts from Biola University and masters degrees from Trinity International University and Fuller Theological Seminary. Dr. Hughes holds a DPhil from Oxford University. He has written several articles on philosophy of religion and was co-editor with Dr. Marvin Meyer of *Jesus Then and Now: Images of Jesus in History and Christology* (2001). Dr. Hughes teaches courses on the history of philosophy, theology, and philosophy of religion.

Dr. Elaine Pagels is the Harrington Spear Paine Foundation Professor of Religion at Princeton University. She received a BA and an MA from Stanford University and a PhD from Harvard University. She was the recipient of awards including the MacArthur Fellowship, a Guggenheim Fellowship, a Rockefeller Fellowship, and recently, Princeton's Howard T. Behrman Award for Distinguished Achievement in the Humanities. Many of her books have been on the *New York Times* Best Sellers list. Her books include *The Gnostic*

Gospels (1979); *Adam, Eve, and the Serpent* (1988); *The Origin of Satan* (1995); *Beyond Belief: The Secret Gospel of Thomas* (2003); *Reading Judas: The Gospel of Judas and the Shaping of Christianity* (2007), co-authored with Karen King of Harvard University; and *Revelations: Visions, Prophecy, and Politics in the Book of Revelation* (2012). Dr. Pagels has published widely on Gnosticism and early Christianity.

Dr. Stephen J. Patterson is Department Chair and George H. Atkinson Professor of Religious and Ethical Studies at Willamette University. Dr. Patterson is an historian of religion specializing in the beginnings of Christianity. His research and writing have focused on the Gospel of Thomas, Q, and various aspects of the historical study of Jesus. Among his books are *Beyond the Passion: Rethinking the Death and Life of Jesus* (2004), *The God of Jesus: The Historical Jesus and the Search for Meaning* (1998) and *The Gospel of Thomas and Jesus* (1993), as well as the co-authored volumes, *The Q-Thomas Reader* (1990), *The Search for Jesus* (1994), *The Fifth Gospel: The Gospel of Thomas Comes of Age* (1998), and *The Apocalyptic Jesus: A Debate* (2001). His many essays and reviews have appeared in *Harvard Theological Review, Journal of Biblical Literature, Journal of Religion, Journal of the American Academy of Religion*, and *Theology Today*, among other publications both professional and popular. He holds membership in the Society of Biblical Literature and the Studiorum Novi Testamenti Societas. He is also a Fellow of the Jesus Seminar and leads the Jesus Seminar on Christian Origins, a group of 150 scholars of early Christianity dedicated to disseminating biblical scholarship to the general public.

Cristina Smith graduated *summa cum laude* from Chapman University in 2014 with a joint degree in English Literature and Religious Studies. She was inspired by Professor Meyer to study religion after enrolling in his course, Introduction to the New Testament, as a general education elective. Cristina was a student of Professor Meyer's from 2010–2012 and shared with him a keen interest in Christian Gnosticism and the *Gospel of Mark*. While at Chapman University, Cristina was the first president of Chapman's local chapter of Theta Alpha Kappa, the National Religious Studies Honor Society. Cristina currently lives and works in the San Francisco Bay Area and hopes to return to school to pursue a graduate degree in the liberal arts field.

Dr. Gail J. Stearns is the Irvin C. and Edy Chapman Dean of the Wallace All Faiths Chapel and Associate Professor of Religious Studies at Chapman University. She is the author of *Writing Pauline: Wisdom from a Long Life* (2005) and *Open Your Eyes: Toward Living More Deeply in the Present* (2010). She received an MDiv from McCormick Theological Seminary and a PhD from Washington State University. Dr. Stearns has taught university courses in gender and women's studies, interfaith dialogue, and religion in America. She is an ordained minister of the Presbyterian Church (USA).

Dr. Daniele C. Struppa is Chancellor and Presidental Designate at Chapman University, having served as provost in 2006 and then as chancellor since 2007. He earned his laurea in mathematics from the University of Milan, Italy. He received his doctorate degree in mathematics from the University of Maryland, College Park. Prior to coming to Chapman University, Dr. Struppa had a distinguished career as a professor of mathematics and occupied positions at the University of Milano (Italy), at the Scuola Normale Superiore in Pisa (Italy), at the University of Calabria (Italy), and since 1987, at George Mason University in Virginia. While at George Mason, Dr. Struppa served as director of the Center for the Applications of Mathematics, as chair of the Department of Mathematical Sciences, and as Associate Dean for Graduate Studies. In 1997, he was selected Dean of the College of Arts and Sciences at George Mason University, a position he held until he joined Chapman University. He is the author of more than 150 refereed publications, and he is the editor of several volumes. He has edited or co-authored six books, *The Mathematical Legacy of Leon Ehrenpreis* (2012),

Noncommutative Functional Calculus: Theory and Applications of Slice Hyperholomorphic Functions (2011); *Harmonic Analysis, Signal Processing, and Complexity: Festschrift in Honor of the 60th Birthday of Carlos A. Berenstein* (2005); *Analysis of Dirac Systems and Computational Algebra* (2004); *Fundamentals of Algebraic Microlocal Analysis* (1999); *and The Fundamental Principle for Systems of Convolution Equations* (1983).

Introduction

Gail J. Stearns and Julye Bidmead

REVERENCE FOR LIFE, EDITED by Marvin Meyer and Kurt Bergel, was published in 2002. Meyer's preface to the volume begins with a tribute to his friend, Kurt Bergel, the first Director of the Schweitzer Institute at Chapman University, who passed away following a brief illness the spring before. When Meyer himself also passed away of a brief illness in August, 2012, no truer words expressed the character of Meyer himself than those he had written. He wrote that his friend

> spent his life devoted to living according to the ethics of reverence for life, and he died a person of conviction, compassion, and love. In this same year of his passing, many have died violently (in struggles throughout the world) . . . If ever there was a time for reflection upon Albert Schweitzer and reverence for life, it is now. We search to find meaning at such times of pain and death. In light of recent events, I thought of what Albert Schweitzer wrote about what he called the fellowship of those who bear the mark of pain . . . Schweitzer observed, "Those among us who have learned through personal experience what pain and anxiety really are must help to ensure that those out there who are in physical need obtain the same help that once came to us. We no longer

belong to ourselves alone; we have become the brothers and sisters of those who suffer.[1]

Marv Meyer would have been the last person to think it appropriate that a book be published in his honor, especially one that celebrates his work. Yet, we learned so much from Meyer—from his scholarship, his ability to make it accessible and turn ancient manuscripts into exciting reads with relevance to our own lives, and his enormous spirit and generous personality that left no one who met him unmoved. "Passionate" sums up the way he lived his life and affected others. Only Meyer could, in a televised interview with CNN, evoke the words, "your passion rings true" from his interviewer after enthusiastically and seriously suggesting that each individual in CNN audience would do well to get into a Coptic language course and allow the text of the *Gospel of Judas* to "open up in front of one."[2]

The *Gospel of Judas* opens with a conversation between Jesus and his disciples in which they want answers---who is Jesus? Why is he laughing? Where does he go when he is not with them? What does a dream they had mean? And the answers Jesus gives are neither completely satisfactory nor easily understood. We may say the same of scholars such as Meyer, and one of his favorite figures, Albert Schweitzer, in addition to wisdom teachers like Jesus. But when we put them together we find true inspiration. Meyer spoke during a multi-faith service at a conference on "Albert Schweitzer at the Turn of the Millennium," held at Chapman University in 1999.[3] In that talk, Meyer noted four ways Schweitzer found to affirm reverence for life. These are ways Meyer himself lived and are deeply instructive for us.

First, affirm reverence for life philosophically, according to Schweitzer's philosophy of "reverence for life." Meyer pointed out many times that foundational to that reverence for life, a

1. Marvin Meyer and Kurt Bergel, eds., *Reverence for Life* (Syracuse, NY: Syracuse University Press, 2002) ix.

2. The Situation Room, CNN, 12/3/2007.

3. This essay was published in an article entitled "Affirming Reverence for Life" in *Reverence for Life*, 22–36.

philosophy wherein one must affirm all of life equally, is reciprocity, a notion found in many world religions, and captured by the words of Jesus, "love your neighbor as yourself."

For Schweitzer and for Meyer, philosophy and ethics included a responsibility for mutual respect with all that lives. Whether fully appreciating the beautiful Sierras while hiking with his family, or speaking to any person he encountered, Meyer had an absolute conviction of the value of all of life, and of every human being—from landscaping workers to colleagues, from students to strangers. Going out of his way to sincerely express, "let me be the first to say," and extolling the importance of the work of the person he was addressing. Meyer took to heart the quote that is on the bust outside Argyros Forum here at Chapman University: *Search and see whether there is not some place where you may invest your humanity.*

Second, affirm reverence for life autobiographically. Like Elaine Pagels in her forward to this volume, many have likened the adventurous Meyer to Indiana Jones, whether he was engaging in fieldwork or tackling a particularly difficult issue in faculty governance.

Meyer brought unbridled enthusiasm to Chapman throughout his 27 years as a member of the faculty. He attended and fully engaged in countless presentations by his colleagues across the disciplines. He served on numerous committees, was the first president of the Faculty Senate, was chair of Religious Studies for many years, and director of the Schweitzer Institute. There are those persons who contribute so much they add to the foundation of a university, and Meyer clearly formed much of Chapman University into what it is today.

Third, affirm reverence for life exegetically. To silence one voice of one student in this lifetime by failing to take the extra time to teach a student until they had the tools to study, write, question, and speak, was unthinkable for Meyer. Cristina Smith's tribute to Meyer in this volume is testament to his endless encouragement of students. Similarly, to allow a voice silenced for two centuries to speak was his profound privilege as he delved into ancient texts.

Meyer opened our eyes to the myriad of ancient gospels as he was moved by the miracle and the magnitude of a most recent discovery he translated, the *Gospel of Judas*.

In this gospel, rather than being the villain of history, we witness Judas Iscariot as a "specially selected disciple" who sacrifices himself for his friend when he turns Jesus into the authorities at Jesus' own request. Judas Iscariot is the close friend of Jesus who is, in turn for this ultimate act of friendship, inaugurated into the mysteries,

> which no eye of an angel has ever seen,
>
> no thought of the heart has ever comprehended,
>
> and it was never called by any name.[4]

Meyer's work spans hundreds of interviews, publications, and presentations—a robust thirty-three pages worth on a vita. A premier and tireless scholar, Meyer was unfazed by the competitive nature of this work. Meyer allowed everyone access to such discoveries, and made enormous contributions to the world, such as when he pointed out that this gospel may counteract the terrible anti-Semitic tendencies of our world. He hoped his research and translation of the *Gospel of Judas* would not only help to revitalize Christian thought about the place of Judas within Christianity, but would stimulate discussion among Jews, Christians, and Muslims on the interpretation of Judas' role in history.[5]

Fourth, like Schweitzer, Meyer affirmed reverence for life religiously, through his study of religion—but, as he would say of Schweitzer, his was not a disinterested study. He was passionate about great music and attended Trinity Presbyterian Church in order to sing in the tremendous choir together with his spouse Bonnie each Sunday. Theologically, Meyer would never be one to say he held any special knowledge, like the Gnostics. He would never be one to say he attained what Schweitzer called spiritual self-realization. Yet we have rarely experienced a person with such

---

4. Marvin Meyer, *The Gospel of Judas: On a Night with Judas Iscariot* (Eugene, OR: Cascade Books, 2011) 32.

5. Ibid., 23.

spiritual fullness as Meyer, whose spirit touched and affected in a positive way nearly every person he met.

Meyer ended his lecture on Schweitzer by positing, "It remains for us, then, to evaluate for ourselves these affirmations of reverence for life . . . How shall we understand the challenges of moral goodness, evil, and ethics in the world? How shall we see ourselves in the context of other living beings in the world? How shall we assume our responsibilities and act upon them in a world of painful and perplexing ambiguities?"[6]

Perhaps one day we will understand all—we will know, with a smile on our lips. For now, encouraged by Meyer's deep passion for life and service, we continue to live into the questions; each of us finding ways to invest our humanity, living every day as part of this fellowship of those who bear the mark of pain, with reverence for life.

This volume is dedicated to Marv Meyer, as a tribute to him as we continue in some lesser way than he to tackle issues such as the ecological crisis, engaging pedagogies to enlighten our students, and pursuing scholarly work in fields related to his work.

In a section on Reflections and Reimaginings, Cristina Smith demonstrates how having Meyer as a teacher and a mentor, stirred the imaginations of students. She illustrates his extraordinary ability to teach and to elicit the scholar in each student. Ronald Farmer provocatively suggests we look in an imaginative way at Christian texts previously utilized to promote a controlling view of the environment, by re-thinking the function of language and interpretation of text. He explores Ecuador's adoption of a Constitution guaranteeing and codifying Rights of Nature as an example. Farmer then invites us to reimagine the relationship between humans and non-human animals from one that is predicated on the "use" of one by the other, to one that is interrelated.

In the Pedagogy section, Gail Stearns engages the question of how we can teach Interfaith Dialogue to a changing demographic of students. Previously, persons were expected to stand within one tradition in order to be qualified to engage in Interfaith Dialogue.

6. Meyer and Bergel, *Reverence for Life*, 36.

Yet today, students are more likely to have multiple or no religious identity. She addresses whether and how we can teach Interfaith Dialogue in a world where interfaith literacy and engagement are needed more than ever as we help equip students to be global citizens. Charles Hughes reveals the careful methodology and philosophy behind an innovative course he co-taught for some years with Meyer. Anyone who was caught between Hughes and Meyer as they discussed their differing views on the subject of "Images of Jesus" knows the explosive effect of their dialogue, and Hughes discusses its dangerously educational effect upon students.

In a section on Ancient Texts, Julye Bidmead compares magical ritual texts from the Mesopotamian traditions to similar Gnostic and ancient Christian texts. She shows how despite the vast chronological, geographical, and linguistic differences in these two cultures, the texts reflect the same societal and theological concerns. James Goehring's piece provides a visual and narrative account of the Wadi Sheikh Ali, Eygpt survey that Marv and he participated in 1980. The team explored rock caves which contained graffiti and ostraca with Coptic prayers and blessings. Kathleen Corley explores of roles and characters of women in early Christian literature and Gnostic texts, particulary Salome in the *Gospel of Thomas*. Stephen Patterson discusses the complexity of Edessene Christianity through an exegesis of several Christian sources such as the *Odes of Solomon*; Tatian's *Oration to the Greeks*, the remnants of Bardaisan's school; and the *Acts of Thomas*.

The volume concludes with an epilogue; Willis Barnstone's playful, yet deeply profound poetic tribute to his colleague and friend, Marv Meyer.

PART 1

Reflections and Reimagining

1

Dr. Meyer: A Student's Memory

Cristina Smith

To say that Dr. Meyer was one of the most influential presences in my life and college career is not an exaggeration. As a freshman far from home, disappointed in the major I was in at the time, I was uncertain about the college experience I had encountered so far. I enrolled in the class, "Introduction to Christian Scriptures," for a general education course with the expectation that the class would be mildly interesting at best. At the last minute, there was a change in instructor, and Dr. Meyer, chair of the Religious Studies Department at the time, stepped in to teach the class. This small change forever altered my experience at Chapman University.

Listening to Dr. Meyer speak was a wonderful treat in itself. There was unbridled excitement when he taught, a passion and energy for his scholarly and academic pursuits that was clear to every student he encountered. He made you want to love, to understand, and to question the subject matter as adamantly as he himself did. Questions posed by students—especially those that were difficult to answer—thrilled him, and he loved the challenge of presenting especially thought-provoking or surprising material. Perhaps the most rewarding experience I gained from that class two years ago was the chance to learn from Dr. Meyer about a subject that he was truly passionate about: Gnosticism. His expertise and excitement about the subject was evident, and had I not taken that class with him, there is the devastating possibility that I would have never encountered a subject that I have become so fascinated with studying. After that class with Dr. Meyer, I officially declared myself a major in Religious Studies.

Throughout the course of the two years I was Dr. Meyer's student, I continued to take his classes and talk to him about the subjects that interested me. An inexhaustible source of knowledge, he was always genuinely excited to meet with me or with any other student to discuss a paper topic, a theory, or even a simple question. Dr. Meyer allowed me to enroll in my first upper-division college course, Images of Jesus—despite my lower-division standing—believing that I was capable of the workload and that the subject matter was truly something that I should have the opportunity to encounter as a Religious Studies major with an emphasis in Christianity. As I embarked on my second class with him, I came to realize what I truly, truly, loved about him and what made him unique from most professors: he encouraged students to look beyond the canon, to look beyond what is traditionally accepted, and to pursue that as a valid academic and personal pursuit. I found myself researching and writing papers on subject matter that was so interesting, and at times fantastical, that I could hardly believe my ideas would be taken seriously. I wrote comparison papers on Eve as a manifestation of the Goddess Sophia, a paper on *The Secret Gospel of Mark*, even a paper deconstructing the demonization of Judas Iscariot. Every time I broached these topics with Dr. Meyer, I was met with excitement, and he did not just look at my work to grade it; he actually encountered students' ideas with excitement and eagerness, developing an environment of mutual intellectual respect and scholarly growth between student and professor.

As an individual, Dr. Meyer influenced my decision to study a subject which I am completely captivated by, but initially never would have thought to pursue. He served as a professor and a mentor, and, unbeknownst to me, the last conversation I had with him was discussing graduate school programs to pursue, with him encouraging me to apply to top programs and assuring me that he would help me along the path of graduate school applications, recommendations, and decisions. As an individual there are disappointments I carry, such as not having the chance to take his Albert Schweitzer class or to hear his personal theory on *The Secret Gospel of Mark*, which he promised to share with me one day. At the university, Dr. Meyer was an inspiration to many students, reaching students of all levels and disciplines through his upper-division courses taught to older students, his Freshman Foundations Course that made him accessible to freshman, and his passion and legacy of the Albert Schweitzer Institute that is unique to Chapman University's campus. It is an incomprehensible loss that he is no longer here to spread his joy among the Chapman community: to teach, to challenge and to inspire students as he did me, to take a real investment and passion in my academics but to also encourage me to push myself to look beyond the traditional subjects and accepted theories. An extraordinary man, he no doubt leaves behind extraordinary loss . . . but he also leaves behind things greater: an extraordinary legacy, extraordinary work, and most importantly, an extraordinary memory among those who had what was truly the gift of knowing Dr. Meyer.

$$2$$

Imagination and the Art of Interpretation

Seeking to Embody Schweitzer's Reverence for Life Ethic[1]

Ronald L. Farmer

MARVIN MEYER'S SCHOLARSHIP EMBRACED many areas, one of which was the life and thought of Albert Schweitzer.[2] For years, Marv served as the Director of Chapman University's Albert Schweitzer Institute. I was privileged to spend many happy hours conversing with Marv about Schweitzer's contributions to the fields of religion, philosophy, ethics, and the music of Bach—but especially the significance of his reverence for life ethic for animal rights and the ecological crisis. Indeed, my last conversation with Marv was immediately after guest lecturing (via Skype from Ecuador) in his course, Albert Schweitzer: His Life and Thought. With deep gratitude for Marv's friendship and scholarship I offer this essay.

1. Core ideas of this essay first appeared in my essay entitled "Imagination and the Art of Interpretation: Reading Scripture and Tradition for the Sake of the World" in *Replanting Ourselves in Beauty: Toward an Ecological Civilization*, ed. McDaniel and Adams Farmer. With permission of the editors, I expanded those ideas in my Francis Lecture (bearing the same title) delivered at Chapman University in February 2015, and have expanded them yet again in this essay.

2. See, for example, Meyer and Bergel, *Reverence for Life*; and Meyer, Desfor, and Jilek-Aall, *Finding Lambaréné*.

Prologue

Language. How much time have you devoted to intensive reflection on the topic of language? If you are like most people, very little. Language, like our assumptions or presuppositions in general, is simply taken for granted. Reflecting on language is a task usually relegated to linguists and philosophers and psychologists, but for the next few moments, I invite you to join me in thinking about language.

As is the case with world views, most of us have unconsciously adopted, by osmosis, you could say, the dominant understanding of language found in our culture. Because that is so, I would like to call upon Northrop Frye, one of the greatest literary critics and theorists of the 20th century, for help in creating the necessary prologue to my discourse on imagination and the art of interpretation.

Frye distinguished four phases of language in the Western tradition.[3] Now, it is important at the outset to say that he was not asserting that there was no overlapping between successive phases or that characteristics of an earlier phase were not found in later phases. What Frye attempted to identify by means of these successive phases was "the culturally ascendant language, a language that . . . is accorded a special authority by its society."[4]

The first phase of language, which Frye labeled the *metaphorical* phase, is reflected in Greek literature before Plato, the prebiblical cultures of the Ancient Near East, and much of the Bible. In this phase, there was little emphasis on the separation of subject and object. Rather, subject and object were understood to be linked by a common energy or power. This sense of connection between humans and nature was embodied in the divine. Reality was unified through a plurality of deities (i.e., polytheism) who embodied this connection.

Now when it comes to language, only metaphor can express in words the sense of this energy common to subject and object

3. Frye, *The Great Code*, esp. 3–30.
4. Ibid., 7.

7

because in the poetics of metaphor, this *is* that. Thus, in the metaphorical phase, words were words of power. Uttering certain words was a sort of "verbal magic" that worked by means of the energy common to words and things.

The second phase of language, which Frye called the *metonymic* phase, is found in literature from Plato to the Enlightenment. In this phase, subject and object become more consistently separated. Reflection became a prominent feature, and abstraction became possible. Logic developed, primarily deduction; thus, the notion developed that there were valid and invalid ways of thinking.

All this entailed a shift in the understanding of language. Words became thought of as the outward expressions of inner thoughts and ideas. Hence the term, metonymic: this is *put for* that; this is a *substitute* for that. Words point to inner thoughts, and inner thoughts point to a transcendent order above, to a monotheistic deity, a perfect being to which all verbal analogy points (i.e., classical theism).

The third phase of language, which Frye called the *descriptive* phase, began in the 16th century, reached cultural ascendency by the 18th century, and remains the dominant understanding of language today. In this phase, there is clear separation between subject and object. A subject exposes itself to the objective world via the physical senses. As with the metonymic phase, words remain the mechanism of thinking, but thinking now follows the suggestions of sense experience. That is, deduction is largely replaced by induction.

As in the metaphorical phrase, words once again point to the natural world—this *is* that—but with a significant difference. Words are no longer viewed as words of power. No longer is there a common energy interconnecting words and things. Words are mere description, mere explanation of the natural world as observed through the physical senses. Words describe things in the "objective" natural world; no longer is there anything transcending the natural world (i.e., atheistic materialism).

As mentioned above, the descriptive phase of language remains the dominant way language is understood today—just ask any literature professor struggling to communicate to students the poetics of metaphor! But Frye felt that a fourth phase of language was emerging. Given society's gradual awakening to the wondrous world described by contemporary physicists and expressed in the imaginative writings of constructive postmodern thinkers, I think safe to say that the opening decade-and-a-half of the 21st century confirms Frye's 1980s intuition. In this emerging phase, which Frye did not name, there is a growing awareness of the interconnectedness of subject and object. All things are understood to be interconnected; everything influences everything else. Interestingly, this emerging understanding is bringing about a profound theological shift as well. Instead of earlier conceptions of the way the natural world and the divine were related—i.e., polytheistic pantheism or classical theism—the emerging phase suggests that the divine and the natural world are indeed interrelated, but not identified: i.e., panentheism.

Not surprisingly, this emerging phase of language highlighting interconnectedness is also manifesting a growing interest in metaphorical language, not as mere verbal ornamentation that could be expressed more clearly in descriptive prose (as metaphor was understood during the descriptive phase), but rather along the lines of the way metaphor was understood during the first phase: as words of power.

Now, with Frye's four phases of language percolating in our minds, let us turn to my proposals regarding imagination and the art of interpretation.

Imagination and the Art of Interpretation

Lynn White's 1966 speech to the American Association for the Advancement of Science entitled "The Historical Roots of our Ecologic Crisis"[5] not only helped lay the foundation for the modern

---

5. White, "Historical Roots," 1203–7.

ecological movement, but it also created a watershed in religious thinking about the environment.

White, a professor of medieval history specializing in the rise of Western technology, asserted that the West's supremacy in science and technology was made possible because of certain tenets of Western Christianity—most notably its anthropocentricism expressed in its exploitive attitude toward nature.[6] Even though the influence of Christianity has waned dramatically over the centuries and no longer permeates every aspect of Western culture, at the presuppositional level the understanding of the relationship between humans and nature has remained foundational to Western culture. Thus, Western Christianity, at least in its Medieval and Early Modern forms, bears much of the blame for the current ecological crisis.

Because the roots of the crisis are essentially religious in nature, White felt that the solution needed to be religious, too:

> What we do about ecology depends on our ideas of the [hu]man-nature relationship. More science and more technology are not going to get us out of the present ecologic crisis until we find a new religion, or rethink our old one.[7]

Christianity need not be interpreted in the environmentally-unfriendly way it so often has been in the West. By way of illustration, White pointed to Eastern Orthodoxy and the panpsychism of St. Francis of Assisi. Indeed, he proposed St. Francis as the patron saint for ecologists.

Rethinking a religion involves the all-important act of interpretation, a process that is as much an art as it is a science.[8]

6. Component ideas of this anthropocentrism: (1) Humans are not part of the natural world. They are created in God's image and have been given dominion over the earth; the non-human world exists solely for the purpose of meeting human needs. (2) The Christian suppression of animism meant that the natural world was no longer viewed as permeated by the spiritual; animals are mere machines; matter is inert.

7. White, "Historical Roots," 1206.

8. Although this essay focuses on the interpretation of the Bible and Christian tradition, it is applicable to all scripture and tradition.

Depending on how the process is conceived, the outcomes will vary widely. For example, some modern Christians, accustomed to assuming that language functions in terms of Frye's descriptive phase of language, interpret the Bible as a rich repository of fixed doctrines and absolute truths expressed in straightforward, unequivocal, descriptive language. In sharp contrast, other modern Christians, cognizant of the fact that the Bible is a collection of ancient literature written during the periods corresponding to Frye's metaphorical and metonymic phases of language, understand the Bible to be composed largely of religious myth expressed in the figurative, polyvalent language of poetry and metaphor. Not surprisingly, these two reading strategies produce very different interpretations. Over time, however, because our age is still dominated by the descriptive understanding of language, both of these interpretations tend to become *fossilized as fixed teachings*, one labeled "conservative" and the other, "liberal."

But what if we conceived of the function of language differently, as Frye believed modern people were beginning to do? What if the purpose of language is to spark the *imagination* of the hearer or reader—to generate fresh proposals about the way things *might* be—not to communicate fixed, timeless information?

The process hermeneutic is a theory of interpretation derived from Alfred North Whitehead's understanding of language and perception, and as I pointed out in my book *Beyond the Impasse: The Promise of a Process Hermeneutic*,[9] it corresponds nicely to Frye's fourth phase of language which he believed was emerging. One tenant of process thought is that language does not so much *describe* a reality as it *lures* us into particular ways of thinking and feeling about it. That is, the linguistic lures at work in a text (oral or written) spark the imagination about what is—and more importantly—what might be. Given this understanding of the function of language, the biblical text becomes a source for fresh proposals, not fixed teachings.

To illustrate how this might work, let us consider the creation stories found in Genesis 1 and 2. These stories are foundational to

9. Farmer, *Beyond the Impasse*, 58.

the Christian as well as to the Jewish understandings of the world and of the place of humans in it. Unfortunately, one of the most salient features of the creation stories is often misinterpreted—or, more accurately, overlooked—both by liberal interpreters who read these stories figuratively as well as by conservative interpreters who read them literally.

This overlooked aspect is a Hebrew expression that occurs in both creation stories (Gen 1:20–31 and 2:4–7, 18–19). The very same Hebrew words are used to describe both human and non-human animals: *nephesh chay. Nephesh* is typically translated "soul" or "life force." *Chay* means "living." Hence, both human and non-human animals alike are living souls; they are animated by the same life force—the breath of God.

The implications of these verses are profound and stir the imagination. Is it any wonder that most English translations have chosen to render *nephesh chay* when it refers to non-human animals by some expression other than "living souls"? For example, the normally bold New Revised Standard Version cautiously renders the Hebrew as "living creatures." The more accurate translation, "living souls," inevitably sparks the imagination. For the remainder of this essay, I invite you to let your imagination fly.

The Overarching Question

Let us begin with *the overarching question*: How should humans relate to non-human animals if they are living souls who share the same life principle as humans do?

The Overarching Realization

This overarching question needs to be held in tension with *the overarching realization*: As Alfred North Whitehead so pointedly stated, "But whether or no it be for the general good, life is robbery. It is at this point that with life morals become acute. The robber requires justification."[10] By the simple act of being alive, every living soul makes a claim on the planet. For a living soul to exist, it must take in "food" of some sort. Thus, life is robbery. This realization interjects ethics into the equation. To put it pointedly: You are alive and therefore you must justify each "robbery" sustaining your life.

— ᑫ —

As I pondered the overarching question and the overarching realization, three groups of questions emerged.

A First Group of Questions regarding Sustainable Development:

To leave space for the other two groups of questions, I will summarize these questions as one complex question. How do we engage in sustainable development that meets legitimate human needs while balancing the need to preserve natural habitats for wild animals?

Western legal systems, in both capitalist and Marxist economies alike, have traditionally understood nature as property. In such systems, landowners (whether they be individuals, corporations, or the state) have the right to damage or destroy ecosystems on their property. Although "enlightened" governments have established environmental regulatory agencies that *manage* the degradation of the environment, such agencies do not have the "legal teeth" to prevent most degradation, because nature is viewed as property. (The reader should recall White's assessment of where the blame for this view of nature largely lies.)

With the adoption of its new Constitution[11] in 2008, Ecuador became the *first* nation in history to codify the Rights of Nature. Nature is viewed as a right-bearing entity that holds value in and of itself (i.e., inherent value), quite apart from any value it might

10. Whitehead, *Process and Reality*, 105.

11. An English translation of the new Constitution can be found at http://pdba.georgetown.edu/Constitutions/Ecuador/english08.html/.

have for human use (i.e., instrumental value). Thus, nature has fundamental and inalienable rights. The Ecuadorian Constitution assigns liability for damage to the environment, and holds the government responsible for seeing to it that reparation for such damage occurs. People have the authority to petition on the behalf of nature to ensure that nature's interests are not subverted to the interests of individuals, corporations, or the state.[12]

The adoption of Ecuador's eco-centric, democratic Constitution was a watershed event. Interestingly, Andean neighbor Bolivia adopted a new Constitution recognizing the Rights of Nature the following year. What is behind this South American—or more accurately, Andean—challenge to the dominant Western post-Enlightenment economic and legal tradition?

First, a little history. Like other Latin American nations, Ecuador suffered for decades under the development model associated with the neoliberal economic system embraced by the

12. The revolutionary character of the Ecuadorian Constitution is apparent throughout its various titles, chapters, and articles, but nowhere is it set forth more beautifully, more poetically, than in its remarkable Preamble:

We women and men, the sovereign people of Ecuador

RECOGNIZING our age-old roots, wrought by women and men from various peoples,

CELEBRATING nature, the *Pacha Mama* (Mother Earth), of which we are a part and which is vital to our existence,

INVOKING the name of God and recognizing our diverse forms of religion and spirituality,

CALLING UPON the wisdom of all the cultures that enrich us as a society,

AS HEIRS to social liberation struggles against all forms of domination and colonialism

AND with a profound commitment to the present and to the future,

Hereby decide to build

A new form of public coexistence, in diversity and in harmony with nature, to achieve the good way of living, the *sumak kawsay*;

A society that respects, in all its dimensions, the dignity of individuals and community groups;

A democratic country, committed to Latin American integration—the dream of Simón Bolívar and Eloy Alfaro—, peace and solidarity with all peoples of the Earth;

And, exercising our sovereign powers, in Ciudad Alfaro, Montecristi, province of Manabí, we bestow upon ourselves the present: Constitution of the Republic of Ecuador.

"developed" nations of the world—and imposed on "developing" nations—that defined "development" in terms of consumption and profit and GNP. Under this model, however, what Ecuador "developed" was the unfortunate distinction of having the greatest disparity of wealth in all South America. The rich became richer while the masses became poorer. And it was not just the people who suffered. Ecuador is recognized as the most bio-diverse nation in the world, a world treasure. Unfortunately, the largely extraction-based economy resulted in one ecological disaster after another, the most infamous being the devastation wrought by Texaco/Chevron in the Amazonian rainforest, highlighted in the award-winning 2009 documentary *Crude*.[13]

Ecuador desperately needed a more inclusive government embodying a post-oil, post-neoliberal development paradigm. Fortunately, simultaneous with the terrible economic and environmental crises of the 1990s and early 2000s, two movements were emerging, movements that would unite in a dramatic way in the election of President Rafael Correa and the writing of the new Constitution.

President Correa—raised in a struggling, working-class family and educated in Ecuador, Europe, and the US—exemplifies the paradigm shift embraced by a new group of Andean thinkers in the areas of economics and politics. Correa self-identifies as a Christian Leftist and Democratic Socialist. His popularity is remarkable when you consider that in the decade that preceded his election in 2007, no less than seven people held the office of President! Correa is now in his third term and still enjoys widespread support.

The second movement that helped bring about the paradigm shift was an organized and politically active grassroots indigenous movement. Indigenous people make up about 20% of the population, and once they were organized, they began to wield considerable political clout. It is from the indigenous people that the most revolutionary ideas in the new Constitution come.

In place of the society-nature dualism inherent in Western modernity, the new Constitution adopts a holistic world view

13. *Crude*, directed by Joe Berlinger.

in which everything is interrelated. Rather than viewing Nature as property, Nature, or *Pachamama*, is understood to be a right-bearing entity that holds value in itself, quite apart from human use. *Pachamama*, a Quechua word, is a goddess revered by the indigenous peoples of the Andes. The World Mother or Earth Mother plays a key role in Quechua cosmology. Problems arise when people do not live in harmony with Nature—for example, taking too much from Nature or polluting—because they are no longer living in harmony with *Pachamama*. They are not living *sumak kawsay*.

Sumak kawsay, a Quechua expression, lies at the heart of the new Constitution. *Sumak* is a word pregnant with meaning: fullness, sublime, excellent, magnificent, beautiful, superior, comprehensive, symbiotic, and holistic. *Kawsay* means life. Thus, the expression is usually translated "life at its fullest," or "well being," or simply "the good life." But the Quechua understanding of the good life is far removed from the common Western understanding of the good life—i.e., consumerism, commodification, and profit. *Sumak kawsay* offers quite a different life paradigm based on four key principles:

- Relationality—It recognizes the interconnectedness of all things.

- Reciprocity—Reciprocity refers to the practice of exchanging things with others for mutual benefit. *Sumak kawsay* recognizes the reciprocal relationship that exists between "the world above" (the spiritual realm) and "the world below" (the material realm); between human beings and nature; and so forth.

- Correspondence—This principle refers to living in harmony with one's environment (social, natural, spiritual, etc.). *Sumak kawsay* is living in community.

- Complementarity—*Sumak kawsay* recognizes that opposites can be complementary. It is a life of coexistence in a pluralistic world.

Sumak kawsay has its own chapter in the Constitution with 25 articles describing the basic rights associated with it. In addition to the right to live in a healthy environment, associated rights include the right to education, access to clean water and nutritious food, housing, work, freedom of association, and access to health care.

All this sounds fantastic—a political embodiment of ideas congruent with Schweitzer's reverence for life ethic—but I am sure the reader wonders, "How's it going?" Are the Rights of Nature being protected? Truthfully, the results these last seven years have been mixed. As one Ecuadorian intellectual sagely commented, "Latin America has a long history of seeking judicial perfection without sweating over enforcement."[14] My experience of living in Ecuador for five years, as well as the articles I have read by legal, social, and environmental experts, agree with that assessment. The enforcement of laws in general is a problem, and nowhere is this more evident than when it comes to the rights of Nature. Although there have been some notable interventions on behalf of *Pachamama*, so much more needs to be done. But this revolutionary Constitution exists; new ideas have been interjected into the grand adventure of ideas.[15] Let us hope they are contagious.

A Second Group of Questions
Regarding Compassionate Eating:

Should I consider becoming vegan, abstaining from all food and other products derived from animals? Should I consider becoming vegetarian, abstaining from all flesh? In the opinion of many ecologists, becoming vegan or vegetarian is the single most impactful action an individual can make for the good of the planet. If I choose to eat meat, which animals will I eat? If I choose to eat meat, will I make certain that the raising and slaughtering of the animals I eat is done in as humane a manner as possible?

14. Quoted in Zorrilla, "The Struggle over *Sumak Kawsay* in Ecuador."

15. For a brilliant treatment of the power of ideas to shape history and culture, see Whitehead, *Adventures of Ideas*.

At this point, let me pause to say a word about religious myth. Religious myths are "foundational stories" designed to teach some profound spiritual truth. They are not to be read as early mistaken attempts at a scientific description of reality. Interestingly, the mythic creation stories of Genesis portray all creatures as vegetarian "in the beginning." After sin entered the picture, people were "allowed" to eat flesh (Gen. 9:1–6), but even then, strict guidelines were established: the laws of *Kashrut*. Rabbis suggest that among the things these laws were instituted to teach is the value of life, including animal life. The taking of a life, *any* life, is a serious thing. Interestingly, in the mythic portrayal of the coming messianic age, all creatures will again be vegetarian (Isaiah 11).[16] The centrality of non-violence in creation and re-creation is significant and merits imaginative reflection.

People from all religious traditions—whether they are vegans, vegetarians, or meat-eaters—are awakening to the need to put an end to concentrated animal feeding operations (CAFOs), more commonly known as factory farms. This practice, developed over the last sixty years, is:

16. The Peaceable Kingdom pictured in Genesis 1–2 and Isaiah 11 obviously conflicts with our experience of nature as "red in tooth and claw." What are we to make of this? "Progressive Christians understand the stories of creation and redemption to be myths—foundational stories that create a framework of meaning, a worldview, for the people who tell and receive them. They're the 'big stories' that make sense of the 'little stories' of our lives. Myths aren't to be read as literal descriptions of what actually happened or will happen. Their truth is symbolic, not literal. . . . the people who originally told the creation stories probably weren't themselves vegetarians. Rather, they cast the foundational stories of creation and redemption in terms of the Peaceable Kingdom to portray as vividly as possible their conviction that nonviolence is God's intention for us. And how could they render that conviction more powerfully than by presenting all of creation as plant eating, even those animals we know to be flesh eaters? . . . The picture of the Peaceable Kingdom is so foreign to our experience that it jolts us out of our normal patterns of thinking. It shatters our worldview and entices us to imagine another way of being in the world. A new possibility" (Farmer, *Awakening*, 62–63).

- Exceedingly cruel. I invite you to read about what life for the 10 billion farm animals tortured in the US annually is really like inside those shiny metal barns.[17]

- Utterly destructive to the environment. Livestock production and consumption is one of the worst single factors in the degradation of the environment, a truth conveniently overlooked even in Al Gore's film, *An Inconvenient Truth.*[18]

- Responsible for a host of social injustices. Think Upton Sinclair's *The Jungle* on steroids.[19] Health and safety hazards abound in factory farming, and meatpacking is still one of the nation's most dangerous occupations.[20]

- Profoundly dangerous to human health. Consider all the food recalls because of *e-coli* contamination, and the growing concern over the possibility of pandemics arising from factory-farmed animals through of the development of "super bugs" because of the massive use of antibiotics in livestock feed.[21]

A handful of countries and a few states in the United States have taken the first baby steps in the gradual elimination of this cruel, destructive, unjust, and dangerous agricultural model. What role will you play in this revolution? How addicted are you to factory farming's "cheap food"? Such food is "cheap" only because it externalizes much of the true costs of production: gross pollution, social injustice to farm workers, increasing health issues, and immeasurable cruelty to animals. Are you willing to pay more for food as we shift to more sustainable, healthful, compassionate, and

17. Excellent (and disturbing) information is readily available on websites such as www.farmsanctuary.org and www.humanesociety.org.

18. *An Inconvenient Truth,* directed by Davis Guggenheim. See the UN report "Livestock Impacts on the Environment" released the *same year* by the Food and Agriculture Organization of the United Nations available at http://www.fao.org/ag/magazine/0612sp1.htm.

19. Sinclair, *The Jungle* (originally published in 1906).

20. Disturbingly documented on such websites as www.foodispower.org and www.pbs.org/now/shows/250.

21. According to act.foodandwaterwatch.org, 80 percent of the antibiotics in the United States are used on factory farms.

honest methods? Remember, the abolition of slavery required a new economic model. Economic decisions are *not* value neutral. Should our actions be governed by expediency or ethics? Should we be concerned for short-term profit or long-term sustainability?

A Third Group of Questions Concerning the Use of Animals

What do you think about the ethics of having animals in captivity? Do zoos serve a greater good by raising human consciousness about the need for preserving species and habitats, or are they mere prisons for human entertainment? What about animals used for entertainment, as in aquatic parks, rodeos, and circuses? What about animals raised for the fur industry? And then there is the issue of animals used in scientific and medical research. Animals cannot sign a consent form, as is required for any research involving human subjects. And finally, what about our beloved companion animals—not just things like puppy mills and dog fighting, but the whole concept of viewing animals as property? Slaves were once viewed as property. If animals are "living souls," . . . ?

Epilogue

> Very little of the great cruelty shown by men can really be attributed to cruel instinct. Most of it comes from thoughtlessness or inherited habit. The roots of cruelty, therefore, are not so much strong as widespread. But the time must come when inhumanity protected by custom and thoughtlessness will succumb before humanity championed by thought. Let us work that this time may come.
>
> —Albert Schweitzer[22]

The subject of how humans relate to non-human animals and the environment is a topic to which spiritual people have turned a

22. Schweitzer, *Memoirs of Childhood and Youth*, 47.

blind eye for centuries. Being awakened to this long-ignored topic is disturbing, especially when you consider how many billions of "living souls" we are contemplating. I will be honest with you: I do not have all the answers. I am struggling with the enormity and complexity of the issue myself. We need to create "think tanks" to explore this subject. In doing so, however, we must avoid the attitudes and tactics of some groups concerned about non-human animals. Compassion must be exercised toward *all* living souls, including those human living souls for whom this issue is not even on the ethical radar. But it is time to begin thinking—and acting. I am convinced that compassion for non-human animals and the environment is one of the next great spiritual awakenings. We need people who feel called to devote themselves to the work of thinking through these complex issues and then implementing compassionate solutions. We need pioneering people inspired by the spirits of St. Francis and Albert Schweitzer. As John Dewey astutely remarked, "Knowledge falters when imagination clips its wings or fears to use them. Every great advance in science has issued from a new audacity of imagination."[23] The same is true in the fields of ethics and spirituality in general and the interpretation of Scripture in particular. I invite you to let your imagination soar.

Bibliography

Constitution of the Republic of Ecuador. 2008. English translation available at http://pdba.georgetown.edu/Constitutions/Ecuador/english08.html.

Crude: The Real Price of Oil. DVD. Directed by Joe Berlinger. New York: First Run Features, 2009.

Dewey, John. *The Quest for Certainty: A Study of the Relation of Knowledge and Action.* New York: NY: Minton, Balch, 1929.

Farmer, Ronald L. *Awakening.* Scots Valley, CA: CreateSpace, 2009.

———. *Beyond the Impasse: The Promise of a Process Hermeneutic.* Studies in American Biblical Hermeneutics 13. Macon, GA: Mercer University Press, 1997.

———. "Imagination and the Art of Interpretation: Reading Scripture and Tradition for the Sake of the World." In *Replanting Ourselves in Beauty:*

23. Dewey, *The Quest for Certainty*, 310.

Toward an Ecological Civilization, edited by Jay McDaniel and Patricia Adams Farmer, 128–33. Anoka, MN: Process Century, 2015.

Frye, Northrop. *The Great Code: The Bible and Literature*. New York: Harcourt Brace Javanovich, 1982.

An Inconvenient Truth: A Global Warning. DVD. Directed by Davis Guggenheim. Los Angeles: Paramount Classics, 2006.

Meyer, Marvin, Donald Desfor, and Louise Jilek-Aall. *Finding Lambaréné*. Orange, CA: Chapman University Albert Schweitzer Institute, 2007.

Meyer, Marvin, and Kurt Bergel, eds. *Reverence for Life: The Ethics of Albert Schweitzer for the Twenty-first Century*. Albert Schweitzer Library. Syracuse, NY: Syracuse University Press, 2002.

Schweitzer, Alfred. *Memoirs of Childhood and Youth*. Translated by Kurt Bergel and Alice R. Bergel. Syracuse, NY: Syracuse University Press, 1997.

Sinclair, Upton. *The Jungle: The Uncensored Original Edition*. Chicago: Seven Treasures, 2008.

White, Lynn, Jr. "The Historical Roots of Our Ecologic Crisis." *Science* 155 (1967) 1203–7.

Whitehead, Alfred North. *Adventures of Ideas*. New York: Macmillan, 1933.

———. *Process and Reality*. Corr. ed. Edited by David Ray Griffin and Donald W. Sherburne. New York: Free Press, 1978.

Zorrilla, Carlos. "The Struggle over *Sumak Kawsay* in Ecuador." http://upsidedownworld.org/main/ecuador-archives-49/4810–the-struggle-over-sumak-kawsay-in-ecuador

PART 2

Pedagogy

Seeking Pluralism through Identity Awareness

A New Pedagogy for Teaching Interfaith Dialogue

Gail J. Stearns

STROLLING THROUGH THE BEAUTIFUL campus of Chapman University in the heart of Orange County, California, one observes numerous busts of famous persons nestled between palm trees, creative sculptures, and artistic fountains. One statue is much larger than the rest and occupies a prominent space on campus, set high upon the steps directly in front of Argyros Forum, the Student Union. Marvin Meyer referred to it as the "biggest, baddest bust on campus." It is a bust of Albert Schweitzer, inscribed with the quote "Search and see whether there is not some place where you may invest your humanity." Marv, Griset Professor of Religious Studies and Director of the Albert Schweitzer Institute at Chapman University, beamed with pride that the bust occupied this spot as the "patron saint" of Chapman University.

Last spring, the bust of Schweitzer was decorated by students with "caution" tape and fliers connoting Schweitzer's collusion with racism, and a group of students held vigils to discuss the issue on campus. The students are showing a growing interest and concern for activism, diversity and inclusion on this campus in innovative ways. This is occurring at the same time as the entire university is involved in positive efforts to create a welcoming campus for all students, faculty and staff. I suspect if Marv had been here to see the caution tape surrounding his favorite bust, he would have shown up at the student vigils and passionately engaged in educational conversations with the students about Schweitzer's lasting contributions to ethics, while also applauding their activism. Today's students are a new generation—insisting upon the importance of embracing a diversity of intersecting identities. I believe they are also calling for new pedagogies of teaching and learning. At the same time, the world of diversity they reflect calls for new pedagogies of teaching the intersections of diverse identities and envisioning a just and sustainable future inclusive of this pluralism.

Marv was, among so many other skills and talents, a master teacher—utilizing pedagogy that highly engaged the students, delivered as only he could with his generous, infectious personality. He was one who reached students because of his enthusiasm—whether for manuscripts ancient or modern. I recall for myself, however, in the late 1990's when I taught a course on contemporary Religion in America, and utilized the text *Virtual Faith: The Irreverent Spiritual Quest of Generation X* by Tom Beaudoin. We watched and analyzed Gen X videos for religious content, a favorite part of the course. Suddenly, one year course evaluations plummeted. The students did not understand the text and could not figure out why I subjected them to these out-of-date videos. According to social demographers, we had just made the shift among college students from Gen Xer's to Millennials. We are in the midst of another shift, this time religiously and spiritually.

Teaching Millennials about the "Other"

I currently teach a course on Interfaith Leadership, Dialogue, and Engagement, a course naturally prone to discussions of diversity in the realm of religion and spirituality. In the past, we thought the best way to teach such a course was for each person to stand firm within their tradition, learn about others through a framework of a short Christianity 101, Judaism 101, and so on, and then find ways to engage the "Other." Our pedagogy was based largely upon teaching about religions and adding insights from the emerging "interreligious" dialogue occurring between religious leaders.

Interreligious dialogue occurs between two or more religions, finding commonalities and points of dialogue that are available while each party maintains their respective beliefs and practices. Catherine Cornille has argued that the best asset one can have when engaging in interreligious dialogue is a "firm foundation within a particular religious tradition." She contends: "The tradition represents a necessary point of departure and place of return in all genuine interreligious dialogue."[1]

Enter a classroom at Chapman University. Twenty-five students have turned the rows of tables into a square, surrounded by chairs. It is the second week of class. Already students know to turn off their cell phones and place them on the desk in front of them, thus silencing texts and app notifications representing various parts of their multiple identities for an hour and a half, so they can simply be students. All sit quietly for a mere three minutes to collect themselves mindfully before discussion begins. Then, students who are interested in doing so are invited to share their religious background or affiliation. As a professor, I am careful to give students permission not to share personal information, yet am eager to hear at least some who are willing articulate their religious "point of departure and place of return," to borrow Cornille's words, as they learn to engage in interfaith dialogue throughout the semester. What I hear is a few students saying they grew up Catholic and still attend Mass on Wednesday noons, or Jewish and attend Shabbat services on Friday evenings. But more common are references to multiple religions and spiritual connections. One student describes her mother as universalist, allowing her daughter freedom to believe and practice what she wants, while her father is Persian and from a long-standing Muslim family. Her aunt with whom she has had many religious conversations is Jewish, and the student herself recently went on a Buddhist Shambala meditation retreat. As the students divulge their religious or spiritual identities, it turns out that this is the norm.

1. Cornille, *The Im-Possibility*, 94.

For some time, students have said they are more "spiritual" than "religious." But what I see currently is not just a statement rejecting religion, but a renewed interest in both spirituality and religion—and their intersection with issues of diversity. Studies are telling us the "nones" are on the rise. But they also say interest in spiritual growth is on the rise.[2] We are in the process of understanding how young people today characterize that interest.

Suspecting that lists of traditional categories for religion or spiritual inclination were not accurately representing the students, we recently began a very informal survey to help determine the effectiveness of our programming at The Fish Interfaith Center at Chapman University with the question, "How do you identify your current religious, spiritual, or philosophical worldview?" Students' answers included religions or denominations, such as Muslim, Jewish, Disciples of Christ, Catholic, or Non-Denominational Christian, as well as Agnostic, Atheist, or Secular Humanist. However, many were unique, such as, "Very Spiritual—Not Religious," "Moderate Christian," "Open-Minded," or the creative response "Jabudhiccan: combo of Jewish/Wiccan/Buddhist."

Cornille acknowledges that some stand in the margins of their traditions when engaging in interreligious dialogue—in a place she calls "liminality." She characterizes liminality as the "solitary pursuit of the truth in the margins of an established tradition."[3] But even this liminal place presupposes a primary religious tradition. She writes: "In order for dialogue to be more than episodic, it may thus need to be grounded in a sense of interconnection that is more inherently religious, or internal to religious self-understanding."[4] Granted, interreligious dialogue in this sense is important if a person officially represents one religion in dialogue

2. The Pew Research Center found a rise in the religiously unaffiliated in the U.S. between 2007–14 in its "Religious Leadership Study": www.pewforum.org. See also the results of a comprehensive seven year study at UCLA on "Spirituality in Higher Education: the Search for meaning and Purpose," indicating the strong interest in spirituality among college students: www.spirituality.ucla.edu.

3. Cornille, *The Im-Possibility*, 73.

4. Ibid., 110.

with another—many statements of unity and communion have emerged between denominations and religions from this type of dialogue. But if we apply the requirements for interreligious dialogue that each person stand within one faith, we are precluding vast numbers of people interested in interfaith dialogue yet devoid of a specific religious self-understanding.

As we seek an alternative, there is another difficulty to consider that many instructors of interfaith dialogue face today. Although they may or may not be mainline denominationally affiliated, a number of young people in American today identify simply as "Christian," which they interpret in strictly doctrinal ways. These students have developed a suspicion of critical thinking when it comes to their faith, following theologies of absolute truth. For these students, the very notion of interfaith threatens the "truth" of Christianity over other religions. These students see themselves as standing within one faith and looking out defensively at "others." These students fall into an "exclusivist" category of Christians as they look at other religions, as opposed to an inclusive or pluralist understanding as outlined by Diana Eck.[5]

In her book entitled *Monopoly on Salvation?* Jeannine Hill Fletcher addresses the question of whether one can relinquish the notion of having a monopoly on salvation when standing within the Christian faith, without being untrue to the tradition.[6] Her approach, however, is not simply to tackle this question. Instead, Fletcher draws the reader toward an understanding of Christianity as hybrid and diverse. She suggests that people can discover overlapping identities with people of other faiths without having to divest any of their religious views.[7] Paul Knitter confirms that feminist theologians have helped him to clarify the fact that, "Our religious self, like our cultural or social self, is at its core and in its conduct a hybrid."[8] This approach is more fruitful than attempt-

---

5. Eck, *Encountering God*. See chapter 7 for her description of these categories and their functionality in dialogue between religions.

6. Fletcher, *Monopoly on Salvation*, viii.

7. Ibid., 89.

8. Knitter, "Without Buddha," 214, loc. 4124. Kindle edition.

ing to dislodge students' current foundational beliefs in teaching interfaith dialogue, and will provide an opening for learning both for those with specific beliefs of their religious truth, as well as those with no set religious foundation.

Turning the "Other" into an "Us"

In order to develop such an approach, we turn from traditional understandings of "interreligious" dialogue to investigate the meaning of "interfaith" dialogue. "Interfaith" is defined by Eboo Patel, Founder and Director of Interfaith Youth Corps (IFYC), this way:

> *Inter*—how we relate to the diversity around us. *Faith*— how we orient around the key symbols of our religious traditions. *Interfaith*—how our orientation around our religious traditions impacts the relationship we have with the diversity around us, and how our relationships with the diversity around us shape the way we orient around our religious traditions.[9]

Rather than "what is your tradition?" Patel often asks university students to consider which religions they have a relationship with. IFYC acknowledges that today's young people orient around religion and spirituality differently.

I propose even further that the process of interfaith engagement does not consist only of investigating the symbols of the religions we have a relationship with, then turning to encounter others (because such inquiry still presupposes an "us" and those who are "other"), but it requires we understand the "other" as "us." Our students *are* the "other," or to put it another way, in our global, digital world, many of us have become the "other" in terms of our religious and spiritual identities. In the past, we sought to teach about religion as each person stands within a religion, in order to engage in dialogue with the "other"; yet today, not all students stand within only one tradition. Hence, if we are to engage in

9. Patel, *Sacred Ground*, 138.

interfaith dialogue, the challenge becomes turning that "other" into an "us."

Even the distinction between religious and non-religious identities has limitations for interfaith dialogue. Chris Stedman self-identifies with the term Atheist, a label that has previously been termed an "other" category with regard to religion. Yet his description of the aim of "interfaith work" supports a method that is not about categories at all. He argues for non-religious and re-ligious persons working together toward common purpose.[10] In doing so, they will "build relationships that might deconstruct the kind of 'us versus them' thinking." The success of this work will be measured on the character of relationships forged between such people, as he calls for "invested relationships."[11]

Incorporating Feminist Pedagogies

These invested relationships take place between persons for whom a multiplicity of factors make up who we are. Further use of feminist and related pedagogies is instructive here. In describing a course she and a colleague developed on Buddhism and Christianity, Wakoh Shannon Hickey points out:

> With the rise of feminist, queer, and postcolonial theories and epistemologies . . . scholars in religious studies have come to recognize that there is no "view from nowhere"; we are all situated somewhere, historically, culturally, and socially, and our position affects the assumptions we bring to any object of study, and the very questions we ask about it.[12]

Not only is there no objective view, but these theories and theologies teach us that every person—every point of view if you will—is itself multi-faceted. Religious affiliation is only one of the

10. Young people engaging in interfaith cooperation through social action was a foundational idea of Interfaith Youth Corps as well. See ibid., 69.

11. Stedman, *Faitheist*, 173.

12. Hickey, "Deepening the Heart of Wisdom," 89–90.

many cultural, social, economic, gendered, and racialized aspects of our person within very particular contexts that make up our identities. Saying there is some essentialness to what it means to be, for example, a Christian (the "us" as opposed to the "other" of alternate religions) assumes that the primary identity marker of every Christian is his or her Christianity, and that all Christians understand that identity in some common way. Yet, as Fletcher notes, prioritizing one's religious identity and claiming that similarity among Christians distinguishes them all from "others" comes "at the expense of" diversity within Christianity. Indeed, the meaning of being a Christian is always "conditioned" by other categories of identity.[13] To borrow a term widely used, each person is formed by a "web" of identities.[14] For example, a Christian woman who is also a mother may find she has far more in common with her Agnostic neighbor if they live in a suburban neighborhood in the U.S. where their children attend the same school, than she does with a single Christian businessman living in an apartment in London.

Religious affiliation can be understood as one of a number of "social series" to which a person belongs. According to Iris Marion Young, social class, gender and religion can be referred to as "social series," wherein a "series" differentiates from a "group." The latter gathers consciously for a particular purpose, whereas a "series" is a "social collective" unified around particular objects.[15]

In terms of a religion, objects around which people relate may include: theologies or doctrines like monotheism; distinctive clothing such as turbans, hijab or Sunday dress; social spaces as seen in mosques or synagogues; spiritual experiences mediated through meditation or praise; practices including specific prayer postures; visual or verbal representations like art or music; or

13. Fletcher, *Monopoly on Salvation*, 82, 89.

14. Ibid., 88; Gross and Ruether, *Religious Feminisms*, 210.

15 Young, "Gender as Seriality," 723, 724. I extend to religion the concept of gender as a social series from Iris Marion Young's explanation of the seriality of gender as it relates to religion, class, and race. She applies to gender Sartre's concept of what it means to be a part of a "social class" developed in his *Critique of Dialectical Reason*.

constructions of gender such as compulsory heterosexuality or requirements for the priesthood.

A person's sense of identity therefore can, by her choice, display the importance of various serial memberships. At particular times, depending upon the purpose or group with which she is involved, her religious affiliation may not be salient—as in the example of the woman identifying more with her Agnostic neighbor than with other Christians at a particular stage in her life when motherhood and neighborhood residence are salient as she and her neighbor join to help to pass a school bond.

A person's sense of identity can have little to do with any of her serial memberships, or, as Young notes:

> At other times she may find that her family, neighborhood, and church network makes the serial facts of race, for example, important for her identity and development of a group solidarity. Or she can develop a sense of herself and membership in group affiliations that makes different serial structures important to her in different respects or salient in different kinds of circumstances.[16]

Disconnecting religion from an essential identity in this way also allows for individual and collective choice regarding how one participates in and lives out one's religious faith—it protects agency and uniqueness. Elizabeth Spelman gave us a language for this in the title of her early feminist work, *Inessential Woman*. Her point was that to essentialize what it means to be a woman has the effect of rendering specific women "inessential" by making any other details of a woman's life irrelevant to what it means to be a woman. We can surmise the same of attempts to essentialize what it means to be, say, a "Buddhist."[17]

The identification of people with religion as "hybrid" and not essential can be seen throughout the history of religion.[18] In Christianity, for example, we need only read Marvin Meyer and colleague's translation and commentary on *The Gospel of Judas*

16 Young, "Gender as Seriality," 722.

17. Spelman, *Inessential Woman*, 158.

18. See Fletcher, *Monopoly on Salvation*, 96.

originally written by second-century Gnostic Christians, as opposed to the portrayal of Judas by other Christians' writing in the first-through-third-centuries that came to be accepted by the church as the canonical gospels.[19] The latter understood themselves in ways that came to eventually be accepted as the norm for Christianity. Yet it is clear that very early on, followers of Jesus understood themselves in vastly different ways. Their identities as Christians would have been influenced by connections with mysticism, Greek, Roman, Jewish, and other philosophies, mitigated by various primary languages, influenced by social, economic, and political stations and concerns, and so on.

Learning from Virtual Identities

One of the most intriguing emerging aspects today of how social series interact toward the formation of identities is the constant interaction we, and especially our students, have with technology. We have many questions about just how, but it seems clear that interaction with technology is profoundly affecting the self-understanding of young people today. Rachel Wagner looks at the contemporary use of religious apps to see how religious identity formation is affected by their use. Most interesting is her assessment of identity as not fixed, both as one engages in online gaming or simply interacts with mobile devices, such as iPhones and iPads, which she notes, "mirror back to us selves that are fluid, multiple, and fragmented."[20] Our individual mobile devices are deeply personal as each person's apps are uniquely chosen, positioned on our devices, and utilized for our purposes. As we interact with technology, we are intentional "pluralists in action."[21]

In *Godwired*, a brilliant analysis of this generation's religious impulses, Wagner helps us to understand this interaction with technology not only affects—but can deconstruct—just how the

19. Kasser et al., *The Gospel of Judas*, 11.

20. Wagner, *Godwired*, 102.

21. Ibid., 105.

interplay of identify formation occurs in all its multiplicity. She compares religious ritual with video gaming. As she does so, the question of the construction of identity becomes paramount. When one enters into the world of video gaming, one moves into the realms of storytelling, performance or doing, identity formation (including multiple identities and hybrid identity), sacred spaces, community creation, world-building, and into realms involving both violence and meaning. These are all aspects as well that one finds in religion. She states of gaming:

> The most basic considerations reveal a shared interest in thinking about structure, storytelling, and an urge toward other realms and transcendent modes of being. In terms of the human quest for meaning, virtual reality is as potent a site for this endeavor as any existing religious institution.[22]

The identity one forms in video gaming is determined by interaction within the layers of technology, rules of engagement, and many more aspects of the gaming context, and can be fluid from one moment to the next. One might be tempted to conclude that this fluidity eliminates any traditional notion of self and identification, thus erasing one's sense of authentic identity. Conversely, Wagner states instead that "What emerges is a kind of natural, if digitally mediated, pluralism that is reflected in the very functionality of our mobile devices, which model for us the ability to live in a state of determined flux." She goes on to state, "Authenticity, then, comes in self-awareness of the flow."[23]

The danger of conceptualizing identity as seriality, as fluid and interactively formed, or should I say the paramount fear it engenders, is that of relativism. Does anything go, then? If so, why engage in interfaith or inter-spiritual dialogue at all? Diana Eck notes that people too readily conflate the idea of "pluralism" with "relativism," but suggests, "the difference between the two is

---

22. Ibid., 10.
23. Ibid., 108.

important: Relativism assumes a stance of openness; pluralism assumes both openness *and* commitment."[24]

Ethical Purposes for teaching Interfaith Dialogue

I propose that the very idea that we want to teach interfaith dialogue, or to engage with religion in the world at all, is an ethical commitment. Our teaching may attempt objectivity in terms of studying each religion on its own terms, but it is not simply relative. There are reasons for this teaching, leadership and engagement.

More than anyone, Diana Eck, Director of the Pluralism Project at Harvard University, has helped us to understand that interfaith dialogue goes beyond understanding difference to engaging pluralism, and has a purpose in the world. It is not enough to simply be aware of diversity and plurality. Pluralism involves participation, "seeking understanding," and "assumes real commitment," according to Eck. It is based upon awareness, but also on *respect* for differences. Noting we are already interdependent, seen most readily when we look at environmental interdependence, Eck argues this is true religiously as well, requiring a process of "interparticipation." Each time we engage in this process between and among religious or spiritual traditions, we affect one another. We become less of an "us" and an "I" and more of a "we."[25] This is not simply an academic enterprise—it is essential to the future of peace on our planet. As we face the challenges of the twenty-first century, it cannot be denied that what we need even more than ever is to work toward "the cooperative transformation of our global cultures."[26]

Understanding religion necessarily occurs within a global context today. Anthropologist Clifford Geertz illuminates the historical shift in understanding of religious identity, and its

24. Eck, *Encountering God,* 193.
25. Ibid., 212.
26. Ibid., 199.

consequences for today's cultures and world. Geertz, whose early definition of religion brought our attention to the power of symbolic systems within culture, notes that our understanding of religion has evolved since William James' influential notion of religion as an individual sensing the "pinch of destiny." Today, we understand through the work of feminist anthropologists that devotion to religion certainly still has to do with individual identity and meaning, but also is public and affects the collective. To understand religion today, one must understand more than a personal sense of transcendence. In a transpersonal way, religion also involves identity, meaning, and power. Geertz observes that so often when we hear of religion, it is about religious struggle, an external occurrence.[27]

Hans Küng opens *Global Responsibility: In Search of a New World Ethic* with these words: "No survival without a world ethic. No world peace without peace between the religions. No peace between the religions without dialogue between the religions."[28] This dialogue entails mutual respect between religious people as well as non-believers for Küng.[29] The ideas that we are deeply interdependent and that religious dialogue is a key to our survival have not only caught on, they are now shared globally. Rita Gross observes that in 1994, attempts to bridge religions toward a universal ethic were criticized as a Western concept at the gathering of the Parliament of the World's Religions. By the 1999 Parliament gathering, the "Global Ethic" was signed by those present in Cape Town, South Africa. This ethic included the principles not to kill, lie, steal, or sexually exploit others. It was an agreement to promote the "values of life, truth justice, and love."[30]

This notion has only grown and is collectively accepted, as evidenced in the theme of the 2015 Parliament of the World's Religions in Salt Lake City: "Reclaiming the heart of our Humanity: Working together for a World of Compassion, Peace, Justice and Sustainability." A common understanding among persons

27. Geertz, *Available Light*, 170.
28. Küng, *Global Responsibility*, xv.
29. Ibid., 38.
30. Gross and Ruether, *Religious Feminism*, 14.

interested in religion, faith, and dialogue has solidified as a crucial component in the future sustainability of life on our planet. In
order to do so, religion is implicated, because for some, religious
identification is a salient factor in the promotion of violence. As
Karen Armstrong observes, what we all have to fear is not individual religions, but the rise of religious fundamentalism.[31] Stedman
presses this further when he notes identities intersect even outside
lines of religion as a force for peace, stating: "...the atheist and interfaith movements actually share a common point of origin: they
both started, in part, as a reaction to religious extremism."[32]

Interfaith leadership, dialogue, and engagement consist of the
intentional plurality in action of each of us toward a more peaceful
world. Interfaith work is essential to the survival of our globe. The
study of Interfaith leadership offers students valuable skills to take
into the various careers, political spheres, and countries they will
work and live in. It may seem to be against academic objectivity to
have such an aim. Yet, religions have never been just about themselves. Spiritual practices for centuries have moved people from
the "me" to compassion for the "we," toward a more compassionate
world.[33]

The teaching of Interfaith Dialogue, Leadership, and Understanding begins with the clarity that any religious, faith, spiritual,
or secular identity is salient in various ways at various times, as
a hybrid, fluid construction. Our theoretical and theological understanding is that faith and religion are diversely constructed
categories that fulfill deep spiritual impulses variously following
historically paved paths and found in multi-faceted cultural identification. In teaching Interfaith Dialogue, we can help students to
become aware of their relationship to and develop a respect for

31. See Armstrong, *The Battle for God*.

32. Stedman, *Faithiest*, 172.

33. One example among many is the way His Holiness The Dalai Lama
addresses persons of many spiritual identities. He urges the development of
genuine compassion as central to spirituality. This includes self-awareness
and awareness of connections and commitment to work toward the right to
happiness for oneself and others. See chapter 7, "The Value and Benefits of
Compassion," in Dalai Lama and Cutler, *The Art of Happiness*.

spirituality, secularity, faith, and religion. This assists students to understand an authentic identity as interfaith leaders, should they embrace such a dynamic role, not as a fixed religious identity, but as people who are continually aware of the fluidity of identity.

Six Pedagogies for Teaching Interfaith Dialogue

I have identified six pedagogies useful in a course on Interfaith Leadership, Dialogue and Engagement. These do not include—but are continually interwoven with—lectures and readings about interfaith dialogue as well as about specific religions themselves.[34] They are far from exhaustive, and may not be all useful in one course, but give a place to start as we teach from the perspective of hybrid, participatory identities, rather than interreligious dialogue.[35]

The first pedagogy is designed to promote self-reflection toward awareness of identity in students. The instructor can create written exercises to encourage students to understand and investigate the intersections of identities as they reflect upon their own social and religious or spiritual location. The students are asked to think deeply about and to write those things they find relevant to

34. Excellent books for undergraduates for learning about interfaith dialogue include: Eck, *A New Religious America*; Mackenzie, et al., *The Heart of Interfaith Dialogue*; and Patel, *Sacred Ground*. Chapters and sources from multiple textbooks are useful for teaching specific religions, including the wealth of resources on religions in America found in "On Common Ground" at www. pluralism.org.

35. I am deeply indebted to Interfaith Youth Corps and the Council of Independent Colleges for the opportunity to attend a seminar on "Teaching Interfaith Understanding" in Cambridge in June 2014. Diana Eck and Catherine Cornille spent the better part of a week teaching and dialoguing with attendees about how we teach Interfaith Dialogue, including one day with Eboo Patel. Many of the ideas for these pedagogies were born, formed, and even borrowed from my faculty colleagues during and after that conference. I owe special thanks to all the participants, particularly Rachel Wagner and Wakoh Shannon Hickey, for sharing specific assignments with me that I have since adapted for my classes at Chapman University.

their identity. Questions they might answer range from reflecting upon their gendered self-understanding, to abilities or disabilities, to ethnic descent, racialization, education, privileged or minority positioning, socioeconomic upbringing, family religious or spiritual values embraced or rejected, and more.

Second, students engage in critical thinking about why we should do interfaith dialogue at all—in other words, discussing the subject matter we have so far taken up in this paper. Students might read and write a constructive paper critically comparing Cornille's definition of interreligious dialogue and Wagner's concept of pluralism in dialogue and critique. Students can engage with Wagner's work and that of other contemporary identity theorists who propose understandings of intersecting, multiple, and fluid identity as normative.

Third, students investigate what it is that spiritual and religious traditions, or faith practices, do for people. For students who do not stand squarely within a tradition, the investigation provides insight into whether the "other" who does stand within a religion is so very different. For students who stand firmly upon specific beliefs within their religion, each inquiry provides enlightenment that an "other" from another religion may identify with that religion for the same purposes these students identify with their own religion. This approach shifts the emphasis from what each student believes and practices as opposed to what the other believes or practices, to the function of religion and spirituality in people's lives. It helps students discover not so much commonalities among religions as common purposes for religious engagement. There are reasons religions have continued for thousands of years, and provided tried and true paths toward individual meaning as well as cultural identity. Students investigate central identifiers of religion—such as ritual, storytelling, community, the search for meaning or purpose, transcendent experience, and rules or authority.

This can offer rich investigation and discussion with and among students, who find they can readily relate to questions asking whether they have rituals that ground their life, or central stories that tell who they are, or places they find meaning, purpose, or community. Some, however, balk at the question, and many claim that the necessity to submit to rules and authority is precisely why they do not fully embrace religion. Yet, as Wagner shows us in *Godwired*, many students are involved in activities like video gaming where the definite and multiple "rules" of engagement required to enter game playing are not unlike sets of rules for entering religious ritual.[36] Students become aware of ways they each unconsciously hand over authority over their actions in many arenas of their lives.

Fourth and primary to a course in Interfaith Dialogue is utilizing a case study method that covers learning interfaith dialogue through traditional research on religion, developing relationships and interfaith experiences, and practicing the process of interfaith dialogue and conflict resolution. Case studies serve multiple pedagogical purposes, including learning the tenets of some religions. Through its "Case Study Initiative," The Pluralism Project at Harvard University has developed a number of real case studies describing situations where religious people throughout this country have encountered one another and attempted cooperation, such as sharing real estate between various religious houses, or trying to solve a conflict between adherence to a place of business and a particular religious practice.[37] The Pluralism Project offers many ways to teach and utilize these cases in the classroom.

The approach I have developed is to allow the students to form small groups, and give each a case to solve. Through this case, they learn a process for interfaith dialogue and interaction which is a key component of the class, one that they will be able to repeat in the future in other contexts. In each case study there is some conflict over religion—be it the placement of a flag, or the right to prayer, or sharing space between religious groups for worship, or wearing hijab in the workplace. As part of this project, students are asked to research (and are given suggested sources) the basics of the religions involved. If their case involves a Methodist Church and a Reform Synagogue, for example, they visit both a Reform

36. Wagner, *Godwired*, 49–50.

37. See www.pluralism.org.

Synagogue and a Methodist Church if possible, interview leaders of each faith, and study the basics of Methodism and Reform Judaism. Students can be asked to work in groups on the cases and even present them to the class, as well as to individually write a paper describing their research and process.

The use of these Case Studies offers the opportunity for students to learn and practice a process for interfaith dialogue. This process involves (1) identifying the issues to be solved by interfaith dialogue in a particular situation, including assessing the situation and learning who is involved and what their intentions may be; (2) inquiring more deeply by researching more about the basic religious beliefs of the parties involved, and concluding whether they are on the margin or mainstream to their religion; (3) discovering commonalities these religious groups share, as well as differences that might make coming together difficult; (4) communicating by bringing parties together and finding potential solutions; and (5) planning ways to implement any agreed-upon solutions. This process is a central element of the course, and can be emphasized throughout as well as on a final exam.

Fifth, students experience relational learning, as the instructor invites guests into the classroom, arranges forums for students to meet with them, or advises them to attend interfaith events sponsored by the university or community. While much of the learning about religion happens through research and reading, interfaith dialogue and learning also happen in relationships. Throughout the course, as students discuss identity and religion, guest speakers can expose the students to a variety of interfaith leaders in the community—priests, pastors, rabbis, nuns, monks, imams, LDS Institute teachers, Sikh community organizers, to name a few. These can be asked to share their own journey and the integration of faith into other social series in their lives. Along with invitations to guests to speak specifically to students, universities and communities often have interfaith groups or events that are planned in advance or crop up throughout the course. Attending these provides opportunities for students to create new relationships as well as to see interfaith dialogue and engagement in action.

A sixth pedagogy invites students to create a project that in some way brings people together for interfaith dialogue, action or education. Students might design websites where young people share their faith stories, invite community interfaith speakers to campus, help organize a response to a divisive issue on campus related to diversity using the five points for Interfaith Dialogue learned through the case studies, or organize a service project among students of various faith perspectives.

Conclusion

Interfaith dialogue and religious understanding are crucial realms of teaching and learning as universities equip our students to be global citizens. The use of pedagogies that emphasize the multiplicity of identity as we study religion and interfaith dialogue allows this subject matter to be accessible to all of our students. Learning about the construction and fluidity of identity and finding common purpose for interfaith dialogue engages students across the spiritual, religious, and secular spectrum. These students will graduate and move on to public school classrooms, business offices, Hollywood production sites, and countries around the world—all places where interfaith dialogue will be needed. Our world is calling for graduates with the skills to become active participants bringing persons with various identities together for the common purpose of the sustainability of life on this planet. Our students themselves, as they sense a diversity around them, are calling for new methods of teaching. Teaching Interfaith Leadership, Dialogue, and Engagement beginning with awareness of the formation and fluidity of intersecting identities opens the possibility that anyone can be a pluralist in action.

Bibliography

Armstrong, Karen. *The Battle for God: A History of Fundamentalism.* New York: Ballantine, 2000.

Beaudoin, Tom. *Virtual Faith: The Irreverent Spiritual Quest of Generation X.* San Francisco: Jossey-Bass, 1998.

Cornille, Catherine. *The Im-Possibility of Interreligious Dialogue.* New York: Crossroad, 2008.

Eck, Diana L. *A New Religious America: How A "Christian Country" Has Become the World's Most Religiously Diverse Nation.* San Francisco: HarperSanFrancisco, 2001.

Eck, Diana L. *Encountering God: A Spiritual Journey from Bozeman to Banaras.* Boston: Beacon, 1993.

Dalai Lama, and Howard C. Cutler. *The Art of Happiness: A Handbook for Living.* New York: Riverhead, 1998.

Fletcher, Jeannine Hill. *Monopoly on Salvation? A Feminist Approach to Religious Pluralism.* New York: Continuum, 2005.

Geertz, Clifford. *Available Light: Anthropological Reflections on Philosophical Topics.* Princeton: Princeton University Press, 2000.

Gross, Rita M., and Rosemary Radford Ruether. *Religious Feminism and the Future of the Planet: A Buddhist-Christian Conversation.* New York: Continuum, 2001.

Hickey, Wakoh Shannon, and Denise C. Yarbrough. "Deepening the Heart of Wisdom: A Course in Buddhist and Christian Contemplative Practices and Dialogue." *Buddhist-Christian Studies* 33 (2013) 38–99.

Kasser, Rodólphe, et al., eds. *The Gospel of Judas.* Washington, DC: National Geographic, 2006.

Knitter, Paul F. *Without Buddha I Could Not Be A Christian.* Oxford: Oneworld, 2009. Kindle edition.

Küng, Hans. *Global Responsibility: In Search of a New World Ethic.* Translated by John Bowden. 1991. Reprinted, Eugene, OR: Wipf & Stock, 2004.

Mackenzie, Don et al. *Getting to the Heart of Interfaith: The Eye-Opening, Hope-Filled Friendship of a Pastor, a Rabbi & an Imam.* Woodstock, VT: Skylight, 2009.

Patel, Eboo. *Sacred Ground: Pluralism, Prejudice, and the Promise of America.* Boston: Beacon, 2012.

Spelman, Elizabeth V. *Inessential Woman: Problems of Exclusion in Feminist Thought.* Boston: Beacon, 1988.

Stedman, Chris. *Faitheist: How an Atheist Found Common Ground with the Religious.* Boston: Beacon, 2012.

Wagner, Rachel. *Godwired: Religion, Ritual and Virtual Reality.* New York: Routledge, 2012.

Young, Iris Marion. "Gender as Seriality: Thinking About Women as a Social Collective." *Signs* (1994) 713–38.

$$4$$

Images of Jesus

Charles T. Hughes

Introduction

I FIRST MET MARV Meyer at Chapman University in the spring
of 1989. He had a jovial and expansive personality coupled with
genuine concern for those he knew. I liked him immediately and
we soon became friends. After all, we shared quite a bit in common. We both came from Protestant Christian families and had
each gone to Christian universities for our undergraduate studies,
Marv to Calvin College and I to Biola University. I can't say for
sure, but it might have been our commonality of background that
formed the basis for the similar ways in which we viewed things
and the value we placed on what each of us had to say in our lively
discussions with each other. We had a few areas of agreement and
disagreement with respect to our understandings of God, Jesus,
the Bible, and the Christian tradition.

However, it was precisely our friendship and the disagreements we had that led us to construct and co-teach a class titled
Images of Jesus. Our similar ways of thinking also led us to put
together a conference at Chapman University in 1999 titled *Jesus:
Then and Now.* The collected papers from the diverse range of
scholars who attended this conference became a co-edited volume
published by Trinity Press.[1]

1. Marvin Meyer and Charles Hughes, eds., *Jesus Then & Now: Images of*

My purpose in this chapter is to offer some brief reflections on *Images of Jesus*, the course that Marv and I co-taught over the years. I will make a few comments on our philosophy of education, including some trends we wanted to challenge and/or overturn, a few of the many areas of agreement and disagreement we had, and how students responded to the course.

The Images of Jesus Class

Trends We Wanted to Challenge and/or Overturn

Marv and I decided that we would do our best to model to students the virtues of sympathy, courtesy, and clarity alongside rigorous debate. Marv and I were both aware that disagreements over religious and theological issues could quickly degenerate into an angry argument replete with name-calling. We both wanted to avoid the triumphalism and self-righteous contempt for religious belief on public display among the so-called New Atheists as well as the uncritical, dismissive arrogance of some theists. If an "education to reality" is required for a quality education, then it makes no sense to claim that one is a high priest in the temple of reason and a guardian, exemplar, and guarantor of all rational, scientific and cultural advances while characterizing one's opponents as irrational, writhing in the chains of illusion and superstition while also opposing progress. Straw man fallacies are cheap, easy, and wrong. After all, self-righteousness, contemptuousness, arrogance, as well as failures to exercise sympathy and critical thinking are all vices that should be condemned rather than modeled. We believed that a clear and sympathetic understanding of an opponent's view is the mark of a mature reasoner and a sincere seeker of the truth. In that regard, one of my doctoral professors once told me that a scholar should aim to to be able to understand and state an opponent's viewpoint and arguments so clearly and sympathetically that it should come as a surprise to the opponent that his challenger doesn't also endorse those views. Marv and I agreed with

Jesus in History and Christology (Harrisburg, PA: Trinity, 2001).

that sentiment, and we both tried to reflect it in our teaching. After all, it is much easier to see where a position goes right or wrong if its motivating assumptions and supporting arguments are laid out simply and clearly.

Marv and I both believed in truth in advertising. We thought that everyone should make their worldview (atheism, theism, religious pluralism, etc.) explicit so that they would not be tempted to speak to their listeners in "code," as some speakers do. By "code," I mean speaking to an audience in such a way as to *hide* your own beliefs and interpretive framework by employing traditional terms (used with unannounced non-traditional meanings) that fool your listeners into thinking that you believe what they believe when in fact you do not. The practice of speaking in biblical and theological code can turn one into a Jesus hustler or a Spirit hustler, i.e., someone who disbelieves Christian orthodoxy but uses its language when speaking to traditional Christian audiences for profit, celebrity, or as a means to undermine such traditional beliefs. The first recorded attempt at Spirit hustling in the New Testament was conveyed in the story of Simon the Magician, Acts 8:9–24. Simon offered the apostles money in order to purchase the authority and power to bestow the Holy Spirit on others. It seems clear that Simon would have used this authority and power to advance his status as a magician and to enrich himself by charging for it. In an academic context, to attempt to use Jesus, the Spirit, or the Christian tradition in various contexts as scams for personal advancement or enrichment was something that Marv and I both condemned.

Some Agreements and Disagreements

Marv is not here to respond to those issues on which we disagreed, so in what follows, I will be more descriptive than evaluative. That is, I will inform the reader about some of our important areas of agreement and disagreement without any real critical evaluation of those positions.

At the start of each class session, Marv and I would state our positions about the subject of the day, respond to each others' views, and then accept questions from students. The vast majority of the time we were able to accomplish these things in accordance with our educational philosophy, which helped us to create—we believed—much more light than heat.

We agreed that there is a distinction between "history" and "theology," but did not agree about how clearly one could make that distinction. In fact, what counts as history and theology, as well as precisely where the two overlap, is related to much wider sets of assumptions than some have thought. For example, historical investigation cannot settle for us whether or not Mary was a virgin when she conceived Jesus. There is much more afoot in the answer to that question than a simple appeal to what counts as history and what counts as theology. Traditional Christian theists who believe in the authority and accuracy of the New Testament answer this question differently than do atheists, agnostics, and religious pluralists, for example.

Marv and I agreed about Markan priority and about the approximate dates when the other three Gospels were written, but disagreed about how much history was contained therein. We both believed that Jesus was a historical figure, but disagreed over how much of his recorded teachings and actions were historical. However, we did agree that there was enough history in the Gospels to reject as unjustified many of the most fanciful interpretations of Jesus. These included the idea that Jesus was a homosexual or a Cynic or Gnostic philosopher, or an Eastern mystic who smoked hashish. We strongly disagreed over whether Jesus could be understood to be the long-awaited Jewish Messiah.

We did not agree about the date or nature of the *Gospel of Thomas* or the role of other non-canonical Gospels in understanding Jesus. Marv believed that *Thomas* was as early or earlier than Mark, while I believed it was a second-century document dependent on the Synoptic Gospels and proto-Gnostic thought. I argued that understandings of Jesus, disconnected from the New Testament, are often so thin or so distantly related to first-century

Palestinian Judaism that it was difficult (for me) to believe that traditional Jews would have paid any attention to him at all, much less mistook him for the Jewish Messiah ushering in the Kingdom of God. Marv believed that the Jesus of history had been buried beneath numerous theological interpretations and could only be retrieved (if at all) by digging through the interpretations to the bedrock of history that lay beneath them.

Marv and I disagreed about how the Jesus/Christian tradition developed and came to be written down. Marv believed that an important element that motivated Christian scribes was *prophecy historicized*, the view that there were scant details about Jesus, so Christian thinkers searched the Hebrew Bible for themes and passages they could use to construct his life and meaning. I argued that this view gets the cart before the horse. I believed that Jesus' followers did not search the Hebrew Scriptures to find things that were absent in Jesus' life but rather to understand the significance of things and teachings in his life as the Messiah. I argued that searching the Scriptures was not meant to fill in things that had been left out, but rather to understand what God had done in and through Jesus. My contention was that Jesus' life already had the main Hebrew messianic themes running throughout it, and so his followers were correct to view Jesus' teachings and actions as *prophecy fulfilled*. Marv and I both believed that the set of assumptions one makes regarding the authoritative sources (memories, oral teaching, and writing) explain the attractiveness or lack thereof in the different points of view that we advocated.

We did not agree about why the New Testament Gospel message could appear to deliver on its promise to forgive sins and put one right with God. Marv thought a Freudian explanation provided a more plausible explanation than a supernatural one. I argued that the best explanation for the experience that God forgave one's sins through the atoning work of Jesus was due to the fact that that was the method that God chose to enact for the forgiveness of sins.

Marv and I did not agree that God raised Jesus from the dead. Marv believed that the grief of early Christians led them to have experiences of the presence of Jesus after his death and that that experience led to stories of Jesus' resurrection. This experience of the "presence" of a departed loved one is, of course, a well known experience throughout the course of human history. I argued that such an experience would not have been mistaken for a what Jews had in mind as "resurrection from the dead." I claimed instead that the language and events that Jesus' early followers reported to describe the resurrection of Jesus was best explained by the idea that God raised Jesus bodily from the dead.

Student Reaction

On the whole, student reaction was very positive and highly interactive. In the course of listening to our presentations and rebuttals, students would typically ask us to further clarify and justify our views. In the course of answering such questions, Marv and I would usually end up in additional debates with each other. The students loved to see that. They not only enjoyed watching Marv and I engage in animated but friendly disputes with each other, but also were drawn into the subject matter in ways that helped them to learn it and to critically engage with it from a much better-informed standpoint.

Conclusion

Marv and I could see that our co-taught course succeeded in putting students in great danger of acquiring an education in the subject matter. We both wished that more courses that involved highly controversial subjects could be co-taught by professors with different—but principled—convictions about the subjects.

Marv's untimely death robbed his immediate family of a great husband and father. From the rest of us, it took a great scholar, friend, and mentor. I am, however, very grateful that Marv and I were able to co-teach our *Images of Jesus* class over the years. We both believed that our course had benefited not only students, but ourselves as well.

PART 3

Ancient Texts

5

Making Magic:
A Comparative Perspective

Julye Bidmead

Introduction

I HAD THE GREAT privilege of working with Marvin Meyer in the
Department of Religious Studies at Chapman University from
2007 until he was taken from us much too soon in 2012. Marv, a
long time faculty member who held the Griset Professor of Bible
and Christian Studies at Chapman, was my colleague, my mentor, and my friend. Though our fields of study were geographi-
cally, chronologically, and linguistically different, as historians
of religion and scholars of the ancient world, we had many lively
conversations about the theoretical and theological commonalities
in our primary texts. One of those frequent conversations led to
an idea that we should co-teach a class on ancient magic and rituals, a research topic that we were both passionate about, and that
was the subject of many books and articles that Marv authored.
Unfortunately, as we often do, we thought we had all the time in
the world to teach our class, and kept putting it off another year.
Sadly, we never had the opportunity to collaborate together in the
classroom. This short paper comparing early Christian rituals with
Mesopotamian rituals honors Marv by illustrating some ideas we
might have discussed and developed in our course.[1]

1. I would like to thank Cristina Smith and Marilyn Love, two Chapman

What is Magic?

Before beginning any analysis of magic in the ancient world, it is necessary to define and describe how the phenomenon of magic is understood in the context of the ancient world. Immediately, this creates a conundrum, as magic, like religion, is difficult to define. Though there have been numerous attempts from scholars in the fields of anthropology, sociology, and the history of religions to understand what is meant by the word magic, most definitions fall short of encompassing the phenomenon.

Early Victorian anthropologists, Edward B. Tylor (1832–1917) and James G. Frazer (1854–1941), with their Eurocentric evolutionary theories, posited a trichotomy between magic, religion, and science. Magic was a lesser form of religion, and a pseudo-science. In the two-volume *Primitive Culture* (1871), where Edward B. Tylor offered his minimalist definition of religion as animism—the belief in spiritual beings—and his doctrine of survivals—seemingly irrational or outdated customs and beliefs that were vestiges of earlier rational practices—he also proposed a linear evolutionary scheme that moved from the belief in animism to polytheism and finally to monotheism. Noticing that magical practices were commonplace among animists and polytheists, Tylor thought magic was superstition and a false science that held no proper place in a "civilized" society. He claimed that "one of the most pernicious delusions that ever vexed mankind, [was] the belief in Magic."[2] Following Tylor, James G. Frazer also rationalized that magic was a false discipline based on a mistaken association of ideas. Frazer reasoned that magic, like science, operated according to rational laws based on causal relationships, but that the law of magic was a confusion of ideas. In his renowned multivolume work, *The Golden Bough* (1890–1915), his evolutionary model moved from "primitive" magic to religion, and finally to his highest form of human belief, scientific thought. He understood

University Religious Studies alumni for their research assistance in this paper and for their invaluable friendship and support.

2. Tylor, *Primitive Culture*, 101.

magic as the "bastard sister of science"[3] and as a primordial stage of human development. Magic was coercive towards the spiritual world while religion, its superior, was the propitiation and concili-ation of spiritual powers. Neither, of course, could reach the pin-nacle of truly rational scientific thinking. Contemporary scholars of religious studies are still saddled with the enduring legacy of this Victorian Age mindset which envisions magic as something unpalatable and archaic.

This line of thought continued with anthropologist Bronislaw Malinowski (1884–1942) and French sociologist Emile Durkheim (1858–1917). Malinowski, in *Magic, Science and Religion and Other Essays*, argued that magic, science, and religion were not evolutionary as Tylor and Frazer had proposed. All three coex-isted in societies, but they served different functions. Science was a profane activity, while magic and religion were sacred and psycho-logical activities, designed to help humans deal with anxieties and fears. But there was a difference between the two. He found that magic was only performed in uncertain or dangerous situations to achieve specific results. Magic was utilitarian, and a means to an end. Religion, on the other hand, was an end in itself. Emile Durkheim, whose understanding of religion was essentially social, asserted that magic could be distinguished from religion. While both contained myths, dogmas, sacrifice, rituals, and prayers, re-ligion was public and carried out for the good of the entire com-munity. Magical practices were mainly conducted in private for individual gain and did not result in any form of social cohesion.

The distinctions between magic, religion, and science laid out by these early scholars are problematic when considering religion in the ancient world. Magic, a pejorative term loaded with nega-tive and illicit connotations for moderns, held no such scorn or dichotomy among the ancients. It was not something negative, forbidden, false, or separate from so-called religious practices, but an integral part life. Magical rites show the ancients' awareness of the interrelatedness of everything in their universe and their way of negotiating with the deities who created and controlled this

3. Frazer, *The Golden Bough*, 222.

universe. Magic, like religious rituals, was a means of bridging the inseparable connections between the gods and the universe. "In its rites, rituals, taboos, and attendant beliefs, magic might be said to comprise, or at least describe, a system for comprehending the entire world."[4]

Whether the magic was communal or individual, or based on what we as moderns might term false analogies, any scholarly definition is too narrow for the ancient world. When discussing magic, Meyer and Smith state, "a more useful and less value-laden term than either 'magic' or 'religion' which one scholar after another is beginning to propose is 'ritual.'"[5] The psychological power of these religious practices lies in the belief of the efficiency and the actual performance of the rituals.

Ritual Texts of Power

Ritual texts of power, like those discussed in this article, reflect the entirety of religious behavior including instrumental ritual actions, recitation of words and incantations, prayers, offerings, ceremonies, and the wearing of amulets.

I have selected a few Coptic magical texts, translated and published by Marvin Meyer in *Ancient Christian Magic: Coptic Texts of Ritual Power*, and will compare them with similar ancient Mesopotamian texts. Despite the chronological, geographical, and linguistic differences in these two cultures, the texts reflect comparable societal and theological concerns.

One of these major concerns was health, including all forms of diseases as well as successful pregnancies. Illnesses were widespread in the ancient world and threatened the continuation of the family line. Spells or incantations were recited to bring about a material change in one's situation, normally the eradication of the disease or remedy of the condition. Often they were accompanied

4. Bailey, "The Meanings of Magic," 1.

5. Meyer and Smith, *Ancient Christian Magic*, 4.

by symbolic ritual actions meant to eliminate the perceived causes of the ailment.

Texts for Curing Disease

Spells for Various Diseases
    (translated by Marvin Meyer)[6]

SOROCHCHATTA
EI (backwards E, I)
EI (backwards E, I)

For fever.
For a pain in the belly.
For a womb.
For molar that hurts.
Seventy diapsalms and seven diapsalms in three series.[7]
7 names of Mary, 7 of the archangels.

This short Coptic text, dated to 300–699 CE, is an amuletic spell written on papyrus. It could be used to counteract a number of illnesses—including toothache, fever, any unspecified stomach pain, and perhaps cure infertility or assist a difficult pregnancy. The simple ritual instructions reflect sacred numerology; three series of seventies and seven music recitations, and reference to seven sacred names of Mary and the archangels. The number seven reflects the idea of wholeness and perfection, exemplified throughout the biblical tradition as in the seventh day of the Sabbath following creation (Gen. 2:3). To abbreviate the text, the scribe leaves off the actual seven names of Mary as well as the seven names of the archangels, who are Gabriel, Michael, Raphael, Suriel, Raguel, Remiel and Saraphael.[8] In the ancient world, names have power,

6. Berlin Papyrus 8324. Meyer and Smith, *Ancient Christian Magic*, 91.

7. Diapsalm is probably a "refrain" or "repetition" of some sort of musical piece, similar to *selah* found in the Psalms.

8. See Meyer and Smith, *Ancient Christian Magic*, 284. Also see 1 Enoch 20:1–8. "And these are the names of the holy angels who watch. Uriel, one of

and invoking the name of a deity or other supernatural being gives one control over such a being. Mary, as the feminine divine and the divine mother, is often called up for protection in these texts. She holds special standing, especially in healing and reproductive functions. Several Coptic texts, such as "The Magical Book of Mary and the Angels," contain spells to heal or protect and are addressed to Mary. "The Virgin Mary thus exhibits the powers and possibilities of the mother and the goddess as manifested in various contexts. Like Eve, Mary is the mother of the living. Like Isis, Mary is the deliverer of those in need, and she can liberate those who are in bondage."[9]

Similar incantations against diseases are found in the Mesopotamian cuneiform texts. One example, an Akkadian incantation text dated to the Old Babylonian Period (ca. 2000–1500 BCE), could be utilized as a cure or a prophylactic for a large number of ailments. Its structure is strikingly similar to the Coptic text, containing an incantation and incorporating simple ritual practices.

Incantation against Various Diseases
(translated by Benjamin Foster)[10]

Congestion, fever, dizziness, pox,
Falling sickness, stomach ache(?), redness,
Boils, rash, tender sores, putrid sores,
Itch, inflammation, bloody stools, dehydration,
Chills, discharge, and joint pain
Having come down from the bosom(?) of heaven,
They made feverish the sheep and lambs.

the holy angels, who is 3 over the world and over Tartarus. Raphael, one of the holy angels, who is over the spirits of men. 4, 5 Raguel, one of the holy angels who takes vengeance on the world of the luminaries. Michael, one 6 of the holy angels, to wit, he that is set over the best part of mankind and over chaos. Saraqael, 7 one of the holy angels, who is set over the spirits, who sin in the spirit." Gabriel, one of the holy 8 angels, who is over Paradise and the serpents and the Cherubim. Remiel, one of the holy angels, whom God set over those who rise."

9. Meyer, "The Prayer of Mary Who Dissolves Chains in Coptic Magic and Religion," 407–15.

10. Foster, *Before the Muses*, 177–78. Goetze, "An Incantation against Disease, 8–18.

Whom shall I send with an order?
To the daughters of Anu, seven and seven,
The ones whose juglets are of gold,
whose pots are of pure lapis?
Let them draw pure water of the se[a],
Let them sprinkle, let them extinguish
Congestion, fever, dizziness, pox,
Falling sickness, stomach ache(?), redness,
Boils, rash, tender sores, putrid sores,
Itch, inflammation, bloody stools, dehydration,
Chills, discharge, and joint pain.[11]

Ancient Mesopotamian medicine included the "magical"—incantations, spells, rituals, symbolic gestures, apotropaic figurines, and herbal remedies, in addition to whatever surgical and physical procedures were performed. Incantations ranged from cures for specific diseases, such as eye and tooth problems, fevers and gastrointestinal issues, or more general ones that acted as panacea to treat a wide variety of ailments, especially if the cause of disease was unknown.

In the incantation text above, the rather widespread catalogue of ailments in the Mesopotamian texts is followed by the statement that the disease(s) was sent down from the heavens by the gods, who seem to also have afflicted animals with fevers. The ancient Mesopotamians had a number of explanations for illnesses and diseases, including punishment sent by the gods for offenses committed by the sick person, the "hand of a ghost," (i.e., neglecting offerings for the dead ancestors), or the result of sorcery or witchcraft, practices that intentionally brought harm. Magic, therefore, could be considered "good," as a means to manipulate or alter a given situation, such as in healing rituals, or could be considered "evil" like sorcery. In the latter case, anti-witchcraft rituals,

11. Though not included in my analysis here, the text ends with two subscriptions. "A)This is a sacred incantation of Damu and Ninkarrak. The spell is not mine, but it is the spell of Ningirimma, Ea, and Asalluhi cast that I took. (B): ([I] exorcise you by the warrior Shamash, . . . Judging God! [Let the (illness) retreat [to] your grasp. You are [for]giving: revive him (the patient), Let me be the one to cast the spell (that cures him).)" Foster, *Before the Muses*, 177.

or incantations for the gods remove the sorcery, were prevalent. One example is the canonical first millennium BCE eight tablet series called Maqlû, or "Burning." Though these texts resemble rituals performed for healing, they are counter-measures for cases of sorcery and witchcraft. Another frequent attribution of disease was afflictions from various demons. In the Mesopotamian worldview, demons could physically influence and manipulate their victims. Often the distinction between magical incantations against demons and medical incantations against personified illnesses was blurred.[12]

The identity of the "daughters of Anu, seven and seven," in this text is uncertain. A similar Mesopotamian incantation against eye disease refers to daughters of Anu who also bring water for healing in ritual vessels of precious stones:

"Whom shall I send with an order to the daughters of Anu,
To the daughters of Anu, seven and seven?
Let them bring to me a [pot?] of carnelian,
vessel of chalcedony
Let them draw up for me pure waters of the sea,
Let them drive out mote from the young man's eye!"[13]

The most famous daughter of Anu is Lamaštu.[14] Her name, which means "she who erases" or "the eradicator," refers to her bringing illness and death to her victims. Though depicted in iconography as a monster with a lion's head, long clawed fingernails, donkey's ears, and suckling pigs at her breast, she is actually a goddess, albeit a malevolent one. The writing of her name in the cuneiform script includes DINGIR, the determinative used only before the name of a deity. She descends from the primordial parents, Anu and Antu, who are said to have thrown her out of Heaven.

12. Schwemmer, "Magic," 428.

13. Foster, *Before the Muses*, 181; Landsberger and Jacobsen, "An Old Babylonian Charm," 14–21.

14. See Farber, *Lamaštu*, for definitive treatment and translation of the Lamaštu texts. See also Wiggermann, "Lamaštu," 217–249; Scurlock, "Babysnatching Demons," 151–58.

Lamaštu is identified by seven different names, though it is doubtful that she is the "daughter of Anu" mentioned in the texts. If Lamaštu is believed to have caused an illness, she could have been entreated to reverse it, but normally the actions against her involve removing her from the patient. The two groups of seven daughters of Anu mentioned here are likely benevolent deities, who are expected exorcise the evil powers and cure the patient.[15] One group could be the seven children of Enmesarra, the netherworld god of law, who is also described as a sun god and who held a seat in the E-sagila, the Babylonian temple. Yet in some Ancient Near Eastern mythology, the children of Enmesarra are the male Sibbitu-demons, seven rebellious sons who are captured by the chief god, Marduk, and are imprisoned in the constellation of the Pleiades. The second group of seven is likely the *apkallu*, fish-garbed protective spirits whose figurines were used in apotropaic rituals.

Either way, the ritual instructions require these daughters of Anu to collect pure water from the Tigris or Euphrates rivers to be sprinkled upon the patient. One question is, who performed these actions? In many cases, it could be the patient, someone close to her, or more likely a ritual expert, the āšipu. Often translated as "exorcist" or "magician," the āšipu was a diagnostician who interpreted the patient's symptoms. The physician, the asû was a healing specialist who also treated illnesses. Their roles, however, were not always distinct, and certainly may parallel one another.[16]

The text ends with the repetition of the miscellaneous sicknesses, a formula that was likely recited after the ritual was performed. The similarities between the Coptic text and the Akkadian one are apparent. They are both used to cure various ailments. They both invoke divine patrons with references to the sacred number seven to elicit help in curing a patient. The healing qualities of the divine feminine are reflected in the plea to Mary and through the seven daughters of the Mesopotamian god of heaven. Mary's

---

15. Goetze, "An Incantation against Disease," 8–18.

16. For a discussion separating the functions of the *asû* from those of the āšipu, see Biggs, "Medicine, Surgery, and Public Health," 10.

bodily purity and holiness parallels the daughters of Anu with the emphasis on pure or holy water from the sacred rivers.

Texts to Ensure Fertility and Sucessful Pregnancy

The continuation of the family line through successful and multiple pregnancies was crucial to survival in the ancient world, though this was not always easy. Fertility rates were traditionally low. One needed almost double the amount of pregnancies to result in a live birth. Labor and childbirth were extremely dangerous for both the infant and the mother. Even if the woman survived the labor and produced a live healthy child, the high rate of infant mortality and childhood diseases intensified the problem. It is not surprising then that we find numerous magical texts related to pregnancy and childbirth.

One prescription for making a barren woman conceive is found in this Coptic text:

Spell to make a woman become pregnant
(translated by Marvin Meyer)[17]

Almighty master, lord, O god, since from the beginning you have created humankind in your likeness and in your image, you have also honored my striving for childbirth. You said to our mother Sarah, "At this time in a year a son will be born to you."

Thus also now, look, I invoke you, who is seated upon the cherubim, that you listen to my request today—me, N. son of N.—over the chalice of wine that is in my hand, so that when I . . . it to N. daughter of N., you may favor her with a human seed.

And, lord, who listens to everyone who calls upon you, *Adone Elon Sabaoth*, god of gods, and lord of lords, if person binds an amulet on her or if (?) someone gives her (?) a chalice . . . or if there is something from you (?), let her be released through the redeeming love . . .

I adjure you by your great name and the sufferings you

17. Pierpont Morgan Library M662B 22. Meyer, *Ancient Christian Magic*, 76.

experienced upon the cross: You must bring to pass the
words . . . that have been spoken over the chalice in my
hand.

This text written in Coptic on papyrus shows the husband's
deep urgency to rectify his wife's barren condition. Opening like
a petitionary prayer, the man invokes the characteristics of a be-
neficent creator god. He reminds God of the role played in the
birth of Isaac to the barren matriarch, Sarah. "But my covenant
I will establish with Isaac, whom Sarah shall bear to you at this
season next year" (Gen. 17:21–22). The notion that God can open
and close wombs is a frequent allusion in the Hebrew Bible. For
example, in Genesis 20:18 we read, "For the LORD had closed fast
all the wombs of the household of Abimelech because of Sarah,
Abraham's wife," and later, ". . . God remembered Rachel, and God
gave heed to her and opened her womb" (Gen 30:22).

Though the ritual action is not specified, the man speaks the
words over a chalice, implying a libation offering of wine. The text
ends as it began, praising God's greatness and asking Jesus to remember his own sufferings.

In Mesopotamia, husbands also pleaded with the gods to as-
sure a successful pregnancy for their wives. In this oracular text,
the husband asks the Babylonian gods of divination, Shamash and
Adad, whether his wife will get pregnant:

> "O Shamash, lord of the decision, O Adad, lord of divina-
> tion: NN, who since [many] days lives [. . .] and does [not
> . . .] in pregnancy so that the heart of NN her husband
> is sore: [with your divine help], knowing (everything):
> will she draw (the semen), will she get pregnant from this
> day until [. . .], as many as there will be, whether (in)
> [nearby] days or faraway days? Will human offspring [
> . . .], will a bone not her own into her innards [. . .], of
> the full time of a woman."[18]

Ishtar, chief goddess of the Mesopotamian pantheon and the
goddess of love, fertility, sexuality, and war, could also be invoked

18. Stol, *Birth in Babylonia,* 36

to aid in pregnancy and childbearing. Here, Ishtar is praised and asked to counteract the perceived sorcery. The structure of the Coptic and Mesopotamian incantations follow a standard format—opening with an extended praise of the deity, followed by an identification of the penitent, a description of the problem, the request for the remedy, ritual instructions, and followed again by additional praises of the god(s).

> O luminary in heaven, capable Ishtar,
> Mistress of the gods, whose "yes" (means) "yes"
> Princely one among the gods, whose command is supreme,
> Mistress of heaven and netherworld, ruler of all settlements,
> Ishtar, (at?) your invocation(?) all lords are kneeling,
> I, so-and-so, son of so-and-so, kneel before you.
> I, against whom sorcery has been done,
> figurines of whom have been laid in the ground,
> May my body be pure as lapis,
> May [my] features be bright as alabaster,
> Like pure silver, red gold, may I never tarnish,
> May (these seven) plants drive away the magic against me![19]

In the Coptic text, the mention of the barren woman having had another person bind an amulet upon her is reminiscent of some Mesopotamian fertility and childbirth traditions. Perhaps this man is referring to a folk practice that the wife may have used in order to conceive, or a reference to sorcery against his wife. His prayer attempts to counteract it.

The use of amulets—ornaments or small pieces of jewelry that gave protection—was common in ancient Mesopotamia and throughout the ancient Mediterranean. Amulets varied in style and design. Some gave specific directions for construction, while others were simple plaques. For example, one amulet reads, "Silver, gold, iron, copper, in total 21 (amulet) stones, in order that a woman who is not pregnant becomes pregnant: you string it on a linen yarn, you put it on her neck."[20] The amulet could be worn around the neck, around the wrist, or hung up on the wall of a house.

19. Foster, *Before the Muses*, 676–77.
20. Stol, *Birth in Babylonia*, 35.

Amulets for healing often contained written inscriptions and/or depicted protective spirits or likenesses of demons, such as Lamaštu. Though Lamaštu brought sickness to all people, pregnant women and newborns were her favorite victims. Blamed for thwarting conception and causing infertility and miscarriages, the cuneiform texts describe her actions, ". . . she touches the bellies of women in labor. She pulls out the pregnant woman's baby."[21]

For nearly two millennia, amulets used to ward off Lamaštu's presence were among the most common in ancient Mesopotamia. This example indicates both the oral recitation along with the symbolical ritual actions:

> 'I am the daughter of Anu of heaven. I am a Sutean; I am teeth gnashing; I am brilliant! I enter the house; I leave the house. Bring me your sons so that I may suckle (them); let me put the breast into the mouth of your daughters.' Anu heard (this), wailing; (the birth goddess) Aruru-Belet-ili (heard this), [her] tears flowing (and they said): 'Why should we destroy what we have created and (why) should the wind carry off what we have caused to exist? Take her and lay her to rest/throw (her) in the sea. Tie her to a wild tamarisk standing to one side or to a solitary reed stalk.' Just as a corpse no longer has [life] and the stillborn child never suckled the milk of [his] mother, so may the daughter of Anu, like smoke, not be able to return to the house.[22]

In the form of a dialogue, Lamaštu proclaims her sovereignty and her ferocity. She demands that Anu and the other high gods provide her with babies to suckle. The gods wail and answer with a rhetorical question. They offer the ritual instructions to have Lamaštu thrown in the sea and tied to a solitary reed, keeping her away from any pregnant women and babies she may seek to attack.

Though the gods are distressed at her words and murderous actions, she is only fulfilling her divinely decreed purpose. In the

---

21. Foster, *Before the Muses*, 982.

22. Scurlock, "Medicine and Healing Magic." See also Farber, *Lamaštu*, 177, for an alternative translation and 224–245 for commentary.

Atrahasis myth, she is tasked with population control through high infant mortality:

> "In addition let there be one-third of the people, Among the people the woman who gives birth yet does not give birth (successfully); Let there be the (female) demon among the people, To snatch the baby from its mother's lap."[23]

Conclusion

Though Western scholars have been overly concerned with the distinctions between magic and religion, it is apparent when examining ritual texts from the ancient world that these concepts are inseparable. The rituals, practices, and words that could labeled "magic" included elements found in day-to-day practices of what the ancients considered religion. For example, laudatory prayers addressed to the gods asked for divine protection or favor, and offerings and vows to the gods in these magical texts paralleled ritual practices in the temples and in the early church. Rituals in general are ideologically-charged activities, and therefore reflect societal concerns. The distance in time, language, and geography between Mesopotamian society and early Christianity is irrelevant—the concerns for healing, family and proper relationship with the divine were the same.

23. Dalley, *Myths from Mesopotamia*, 35.

Bibliography

Bailey, Michael. "The Meanings of Magic." *Magic, Ritual, and Witchcraft* 1 (Summer 2006) 1–23.

Biggs, Robert D. "ŠA.ZI.GA and the Babylonian Sexual Potency Text." *Comptes rendus des séances de l'Académie des Inscriptions et Belles-Lettres* 47 (2001) 71–78.

———. "Medicine, Surgery, and Public Health in Ancient Mesopotamia." *Journal of Assyrian Academic Studies* 19 (2005) 1–19.

Chavalas, Mark W. *Women in the Ancient Near East: A Sourcebook*. New York: Routledge, 2013.

Cunningham, Graham. *Religion and Magic: Approaches and Theories*. New York: New York University Press, 1999.

Dalley, Stephanie. *Myths from Mesopotamia*. Rev. ed. Oxford: Oxford University Press, 2009.

Durkheim, Emile. *The Elementary Forms of Religious Life*. Translated by Karen E. Fields. NewYork: Free Press, 1995.

Farber, Gertrude. "Another Old Babylonian Childbirth Incantation." *Journal of Near Eastern Studies* 43 (1984) 311–16.

Farber, Walter. *Lamaštu: An Edition of the Canonical Series of Lamaštu Incantations and Rituals and Related Texts from the Second and First Millennia BC*. Winona Lake, IN: Eisenbrauns, 2014.

Foster, Benjamin R. *Before the Muses: An Anthology of Akkadian Literature*. 3rd ed. Bethesda, MD: CDL, 2005.

Frazer, James G. *The Golden Bough: A Study of Magic and Religion*. Edited by Robert Fraser. World's Classics. Oxford: Oxford University Press, 1994.

Goetze, Albrecht. "An Incantation against Disease." *Journal of Cuneiform Studies* 9 (1955) 8–18.

Landsberger, Benno, and Thorkild Jacobsen. "An Old Babylonian Charm against Merḫu." *Journal of Near Eastern Studies* 14 (1955) 14–21.

Malinowski, Bronislaw. *Magic, Science and Religion and Other Essays*. Boston: Beacon, 1948.

Meyer, Marvin. "The Prayer of Mary Who Dissolves Chains in Coptic Magic and Religion." In *Magic and Ritual in the Ancient World*, edited by Paul Allan Mirecki and Marvin W. Meyer, 407–15. Leiden: Brill, 2002.

Meyer, Marvin, and Paul Allan Mirecki. *Magic and Ritual in the Ancient World*. Leiden: Brill, 2002.

Meyer, Marvin, and Richard Smith, eds. *Ancient Christian Magic: Coptic Texts of Ritual Power*. San Francisco: HarperCollins, 1994; new ed. Princeton: Princeton University Press, 1999.

Schwemer, Daniel. "Magic Rituals: Conceptualization and Performance." In *The Oxford Handbook of Cuneiform Culture*, by Karen Radner and Eleanor Robson, 418–42. Oxford: Oxford University Press, 2011.

Scurlock, JoAnn. "Medicine and Healing Magic." In *Women in the Ancient Near East: A Sourcebook*, by Mark W. Chavalas, 101–43. London: Routledge, 2013.

———. "Baby-snatching Demons, Restless Souls and the Dangers of Childbirth: Medico-Magical Means of Dealing with Some of the Perils of Motherhood in Ancient Mesopotamia." *Incognita* 2 (1991) 135–83.

Stol, M. *Birth in Babylonia and the Bible: Its Mediterranean Setting.* Cuneiform Monographs 14. Groningen: Styx, 2000.

Tambiah, Stanley Jeyaraja. *Magic, Science and Religion and the Scope of Rationality.* Lewis Henry Morgan Lectures 1984. Cambridge: Cambridge University Press, 1990.

Tylor, Edward Burnett. *Primitive Culture: Researches into the Development of Mythology, Philosophy, Religion, Art, and Customs.* 2 vols. 1871. Reprinted, New York: Harper, 1958.

Wiggermann, Frans A. M. "Lamaštu, Daughter of Anu: A Profile." In *Birth in Babylonia and the Bible: Its Mediterranean Setting*, by M. Stol, 217–49. Cuneiform Monographs 14. Groningen: Styx, 2000.

—————— 6 ——————

Exploring the Wadi Sheikh Ali

Photographic Evidence from the 1980 Survey

————— *James E. Goehring* —————

NOSTALGIA AND SADNESS ACCOMPANY me as I write this brief account of the Wadi Sheikh Ali survey conducted in December 1980 by a small team from the now defunct Institute for Antiquity and Christianity of Claremont, California. Led by a local guide and accompanied by an Egyptian inspector of antiquities, the three members of the survey team included Marvin Meyer and myself from Claremont Graduate University, and Gary Lease from the University of California at Santa Cruz. Gary passed away on January 4, 2008 and Marvin followed some four years later on August 16, 2012. Both died young. In reviewing my photographs and notes for this piece, I found myself reliving the fun we had together on the survey and more generally in the Nag Hammadi excavations. As I composed the following, I came to appreciate again Marv's and Gary's adventurous side, a side that both nurtured together with their scholarship throughout their lives. It is difficult for me to accept that I write now as the sole surviving western member of the survey team. In this connection, as a contribution to a volume dedicated to the memory of Marvin Meyer, I dedicate my essay to Marv and Gary. We were friends then, and in the context of this essay, it seems fitting to honor them together now. Marv would have wanted it that way. The Wadi Sheikh Ali survey formed part of a

series of investigations planned for the December 1980 season of
the Claremont Nag Hammadi Excavations, a season when actual
digging at Faw Qibli, the site of the central Pachomian monastery
of Pbow, did not occur. The other major goal of the season involved a survey of the nearby village of al-Qasr (ancient Šeneset)
and the adjacent Monastery of Palamon.[1] Knowledge of the Wadi
Sheikh Ali site had come to James Robinson in an earlier season
through local contacts, who described a location some distance up
the ravine where numerous incised and painted Coptic inscriptions could be found. A subsequent visit by Robinson led to the
site's inclusion in the 1980 survey plans with the aim of gathering
more detailed information on the inscriptions and their setting.[2]
Sandwiched between the survey of al-Qasr and a hike up the face
of the Jabal al-Tarif to the eastern desert plateau, the Wadi Sheikh
Ali survey proved the most intriguing of the various investigations conducted that winter. Five individuals participated: our local guide, Munir al-Qummus Basilyus, the Egyptian antiquities
inspector, Rabia Ahmed Hamid, and Marv, Gary, and I. A sixth
individual from the immediate area accompanied us as a guard,
armed with the requisite rifle for protection from serpents, we
were told. Preliminary reports of the investigation of the Wadi
Sheikh Ali have been published by Marvin Meyer, and in the early
years following the survey, we often spoke together of a return trip
during which we would better document the site and eventually
publish it. Life, however, intervened, and that trip never materialized. What follows derives from my notes and memories, Meyer's
published accounts,[3] and the numerous photographs that I took

1. Beebe and Meyer, "Literary and Archaeological Survey of al-Qasr,"
25–29 with two plates. The season also included a hike up the face of the Jabal
al-Tarif and a brief visit to the el-Malak Monastery in el-Rahmaniya Qibli.

2. Meyer, "Archaeological Survey of the Wadi Sheikh Ali: December 1980,"
77; Meyer, "Wadi Sheikh Ali Survey, December 1980," 22. Robinson's visit
served more as reconnaissance, which led to the desire for more specific information. A photograph of Robinson inspecting inscriptions in the Wadi Sheikh
Ali appears in the Claremont Colleges Digital Library.

3. Meyer, "Archaeological Survey," 77–82; Meyer, "Wadi Sheikh Ali Survey," 22–24; Meyer, "Wādī Shaykh ʾAlī," 7.2312–13. A brief account of the

during the 1980 survey.[4] It offers, in a sense, a pictorial guide to Meyer's reports.

The Wadi Sheikh Ali emerges from the rising cliffs of the eastern plateau into the desert of the Dishna plain some 5 km. NNW of the village of Abū Manna, which lies in turn some 22 km. NE of Nag Hammadi. As our party drove across the Dishna plain towards the mouth of the wadi, we could see the sheer face of the massive Jabal al-Tarif, at the base of which the Nag Hammadi codices were found, rising in the distance to the west, as well as that of the similar closer cliffs of the Jabal abū Manna to the east.[5] The wandering route taken by our jeep across the Dishna plain from the Abū Manna-Bahari crossroads to the mouth of the Wadi Sheikh Ali covered some four kilometers along sometimes visible paths that one might call roads, though the bouncing and shuddering of the vehicle suggested otherwise. The mouth of the Wadi Sheikh Ali, actually a double mouth that led back up two distinct ravines, emerged as we drew closer. Our guide identified the Wadi Sheikh Ali as the one on the left, an impressive rugged cut slicing back into the cliffs.

---

survey appeared earlier in the *Bulletin of the Institute for Antiquity and Christianity* 8.1 (1981) 8–10. I also wrote a short article, "Sheikh Ali, Wadi," which is yet to appear.

4. A few additional black-and-white photographs of the Wadi Sheikh Ali are available on the Claremont Colleges Digital Library website (http://ccdl. libraries.claremont.edu/), and I suspect more may exist in the Nag Hammadi Archive, though I have not consulted the archive or incorporated any of the Claremont photographs in this paper. The fact that one of the photographs in the digital library depicts James Robinson inspecting inscriptions suggests their connection with Robinson's earlier reconnaissance of the site.

5. Meyer, "Archaeological Survey," 77; "Wādī Shaykh 'Alī," 2312.

The Mouth of the Wadi Sheikh Ali viewed from the Dishna Plain.
Marvin Meyer is at the back, and Gary Lease is to his right wearing a hat.
All photos in this chapter are courtesy of the author, James E. Goehring

It led into a rugged ravine bordered by limestone cliffs that, judging from maps, extends some five to six kilometers back rising up into the plateau. Given its northerly direction and size, it does not appear to have functioned as an overland route to the Red Sea. We followed a relatively good path up the ravine, clamoring over rocks as we went. We marveled at the natural grandeur of the place filled with large boulders and abutted on either side by sheer cliffs of immense size. Vistas looking back into the wadi reminded me of walled canyons that I had hiked in the southwest. Myriad round limestone concretions were visible imbedded in the cliffs' walls and more were strewn across the wadi floor where they fell as the cliffs eroded. Among them were numerous fossilized sea shells, mostly clams, though Marv's sharp eyes picked out a small sea urchin as well.[6]

6. Meyer, "Archaeological Survey," 77–78; Meyer, "Wādī Shaykh ʾAlī," 2312.

The Wadi Sheikh Ali

Approximately one and a half kilometers into the wadi, about half way to our destination, Munir, our guide, pointed to a large boulder that had been in the process of being cut or quarried in antiquity. It lay in the middle of the ravine. Two parallel rows marking the intended cut ran across the top of the slab, on one side, a long series of deep short rectangular cuts, and on the other, a parallel—though much less defined—depression in the stone. The pattern suggested an unfinished obelisk, perhaps abandoned by the workers when it broke unexpectedly. We noted numerous Byzantine era shards in the area, but as the visitation site remained our primary goal, we chose not to explore the area for further evidence of quarrying activity.[7]

7. Meyer, "Archaeological Survey," 78; Meyer, "Wādī Shaykh ʾAlī," 7.2312; Meyer, "Wadi Sheiklh Ali Survey," 23.

The unfinished obelisk

An additional one and a half kilometer hike further into the ravine brought us to our destination, the visitation site. Munir first pointed to a large square shaped boulder on which numerous inscriptions occurred, both scratched into the rock (graffiti) and written on it in red paint (dipinti), identified jokingly by Marv as monastic rustoleum. The pious inscriptions on the boulder were all from the Coptic era, written ostensibly by monks, variously identifying themselves, calling on God, and asking to be remembered in prayer.

A short distance further up, the wadi the cliffs on the left side rise dramatically. A long, deep overhang extends along their base, cut by erosion and filled with evidence of human visitation and/or occupation.[8]

---

8. For Meyer's account of this entire area and its inscriptions, see Meyer "Archaeological Survey"; Meyer, "Wadi Sheiklh Ali Survey"; and Meyer, "Wādī Shaykh ʾAlī."

The visitation site with the large square shaped boulder visible
in the distance to the left of the outcropping

Marvin Meyer with our local guide and the antiquities
inspector checking out the central overhang

At its deepest, the overhang reaches five to six meters back into the cliff, though partially blocked at this point by a large boulder. The area was covered with Coptic era inscriptions (dipinti and graffiti), as well as a few roughly drawn hieroglyphs, images of Egyptian figures, an ankh, and primitive incised drawings of boats, hunters, and animals (ibex, lion, ram, birds, and fish). A cartouche of the pharaoh Menkaure appears,[9] and one scene includes the god Min. In another, one sees "a lion, with mane, . . . attacking a hunter, with spear; the lion appears to be overcoming the hunter."[10] The boats have raised bows and sterns with banks of oars extending along the side. In a few, human figures can be seen towards the stern, apparently steering or poling the boat forward. In addition, at least two examples of a thatch-like square with a square opening in the middle occur, perhaps representing hunting traps or enclosures.[11]

Cartouche of Menkaure and the hieroglyph for "gods"

9. Meyer, "Archaeological Survey," 81; Meyer, "Wadi Sheiklh Ali Survey," 23; Meyer, "Wādī Shaykh ʾAlī," 2313.

10. Meyer, "Archaeological Survey," 81; Meyer, "Wādī Shaykh ʾAlī," 2313

11. For the boats and hunting enclosures, see Meyer, "Archaeological Survey," 81; Meyer, "Wadi Sheiklh Ali Survey," 23; Meyer, "Wādī Shaykh ʾAlī," 2313.

Graffiti of Egyptian figures

Graffiti of boats with oars and poles

Lion and Coptic graffiti

The Coptic era dipinti and graffiti that cover the rock walls include typical Coptic crosses and pious requests for remembrance and prayer.[12] The latter, which correspond to examples from other known sites,[13] typically identify the petitioner who asks to be remembered or prayed for in love. Individual inscriptions occasionally include crosses, self-deprecating statements, a relational identification (son of, etc.), and the petitioner's or his father's occupation or office. The latter include apa, deacon or servant, and oil dealer. Many are damaged and thus incomplete and/or difficult to read. One can only assume that their deterioration has continued in the ensuing years. The following offer typical examples.[14]

12. Examples appear in Meyer, "Archaeological Survey," 78–79; Meyer, "Wadi Sheiklh Ali Survey," 22–23; Meyer, "Wādī Shaykh ʾAlī," 2312.

13. Yassâ, Till, and Khs-Burmeister, "Coptic Grafitti and Inscritpions from the Monastery of Phoebammon," 21–102 and plates iii–v; Crum and Evelyn-White, *Monastery of Epiphanius at Thebes*, 141–43, 379–82.

14. The Coptic transliteration follows that found in Layton, *Coptic Grammar*, 13.

+ šlēl ečoi nagapē
+ Pray for me in love.

anok {pkhm̥ hl} pakire
I am your servant, Pakire.

+ anok khaēl perefrnobe
+ I am Chael the sinner.

aritakape šlēl
Please pray

ečoi . . .
For me

aripamewe afilō[theos] pšēre
Remember Philotheos Son

nagapē ndaweid
in love. of David

anok foibamōn
I am Phoibamon,

pšēnfilothios
the son of Philotheos

ps·anneh
the oil dealer.

anok abraham
I am Abraham,

ptiakōnos
the deacon.

aripamewe nakapē anok
Remember me in love. I

perefernabe para rome
am the one who sins amore

nim pčoeis erof o
than all

nae m̄ñtapsēkhē
men. May the Lord have

anok apa pšēre
mercy on my soul.

I am Apa Pshere

Various individuals appear multiple times. Philotheos, son of David, requests to be remembered in at least three separate inscriptions, and Phoibamon, the son of the oil dealer Philotheos, incised his name into the rocks at least twice. One suspects that a careful investigation of the site would reveal additional figures with multiple prayer requests.

Coptic Dipinti
The request by Chael appears in the center

Coptic dipinti of Apa Pshere

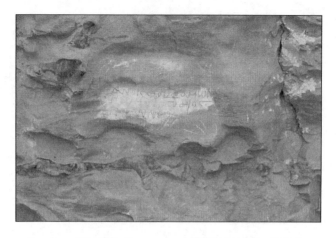

Coptic graffiti of Phoibamon, son of Philotheos the oil dealer

Coptic graffiti

In addition to the dipinti painted on the rock walls, I picked up a small limestone shard (19 x 7 cm) beneath the central over-hang inscribed with the words (in red paint) "I am Archeleos.

Please remember me."[15] As the words wrap around to the side of the rock fragment, it appears that it was inscribed after it had broken off of the cliff.[16]

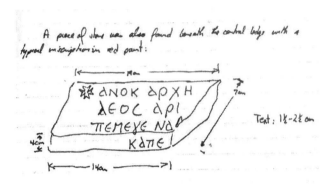

Rough notebook drawing of inscribed limestone shard

Perhaps the most fascinating graffito from this period, incised in the cliff, is that of a bearded and robed figure, most likely a monk, with his arms raised in prayer. The accompanying inscription read "I am John, the shoemaker" (anok iōhannēs pkēse).[17]

15. Cited in Meyer, "Archaeological Survey," 79–80; Meyer, "Wadi Sheiklh Ali Survey," 22–23; idem, "Wādī Shaykh 'Alī," 7.2312.

16. One might note also that the writer began writing the k in *nakape* on the upper flat surface and failing to have room to complete it, moved to the side of the stone shard to complete it.

17. Meyer ("Archaeological Survey," 80; Meyer, "Wādī Shaykh 'Alī," 2313) reads *anok iōhannēs pkēse* and translates "'I am faithful John' or 'I, John, am faithful.'" The reading *pkēse* (the shoemaker), which is surely correct, was suggested by Lance Jennot in an email of April 20, 2015, after I shared photographs of the graffito with him and Hugo Lundhaug for use in an upcoming volume. He noted further the inclusion of shoemaker as one of the occupations of the Pachomian monks mentioned by Palladius in his *Lausiac History* 32.12. At least one additional example of the inclusion of an occupation in the inscription occurs in the wadi, namely that of "Phoibamon, the son of Philotheos the oil dealer" (see above). For a somewhat similar depiction of a monk named "Misaêl (the) humble," see al-Mâsiḥ, Till, and Burmeister, "Coptic Grafitti and Inscriptions from the Monastery of Phoebammon," plate V (inscription no. 179).

Incised figure of the monk John[18]

While the inscriptions are predominantly in Coptic and probably from the Byzantine era, at least one inscription in Greek[19] and several in Arabic occur. Two of the latter, in black paint, are modern,[20] and a third may date to the tenth century according to our Egyptian Antiquities Inspector, Rabia Ahmed Hamid. In addition to the numerous inscriptions, a large number of Roman era bricks were scattered around the area, one of which Gary Lease identified as from a brick oven. Numerous potsherds were also lying about. Most were identified as Byzantine ware, though Roman and Islamic era sherds also occurred. A number of the Roman period pieces were decorated with patterns similar to that of the so-called lid of the jar in which the Nag Hammadi codices were found. In addition, Keith Beebe later suggested that one beauti-

18. The photograph was used on the cover of my *Ascetics, Society, and the Desert.* The drawing, which I produced, appeared in the *Bulletin of the Institute for Antiquity and Christianity,* 9; Meyer, "Archeological Survey," 80; Meyer, "Wadi Sheikh Ali Survey," 24; and on the cover of the Program of the 2004 annual meeting of the North American Patristics Society.

19. Greek inscriptions likewise occur along with the Coptic ones at the Monastery of Phoebammon and the Monastery of Epiphanius at Thebes. See Rémondon, "Graffiti Grecs du Monastère de Phoebammon"; Crum and Evelyn-White, *The Monastery of Epiphanius at Thebes,* 144–47, 383–86.

20. These inscriptions name, according to our antiquities inspector, a person from Faw Qibli.

fully decorated sherd that we brought back and showed to him looked like Nabetean ware. This piece and the inscribed limestone sherd remained in the possession of our Egyptian Antiquities Inspector for transfer to the Coptic museum.

Roman era bricks in front of the overhang site

The protective nature of the overhang around which the graffiti and dipinti congregate suggests the origin of its use. The rugged landscape through which one traveled up and down the wadi offers little respite from the sun and its heat. The extended overhang offered the only reliable place to withdraw from such exposure in the section of the wadi we traversed. It offered a place to rest, store one's supplies (water) out of the reach of the sun, and perhaps sleep comfortably. Such would fit the tentative scenario Meyer offered for the use of wadi and overhang site. He wrote:

> Early stonecutters and quarries may have used the wadi (confirmed by the obelisk and worked stone seen in the wadi). Hunters naturally would accompany them, and could have scratched typical hunting graffiti onto the

western face of the wadi cliff, where the overhang would supply shady relief from the afternoon sun and perhaps shelter in the evening. Many centuries later, we would suggest, Coptic monks must have happened upon the scenes and hieroglyphs, and rededicated the site in their usual fashion by means of Christian graffiti, while possibly using it for pilgrimage or retreat. Whether or not a substantial installation, or even a burial of a holy personage, existed at the Coptic site is impossible to say without further exploration.[21]

The various elements in the scenario all make sense, though they remain hypotheses in need of further exploration and study. The cartouche of Menkare, together with the other hieroglyphs and images of Egyptian deities, certainly suggests pharaonic usage of the wadi, as does the unfinished obelisk.[22] While hunters attending those doing the stone cutting likewise could explain some of the depictions, one can imagine an alternative scenario in which the stonecutters themselves (or those who attended them) scratched the boats and animal scenes into the cliffs as they retired in the evening, drawing on their memories of the valley and the various animals and images that they had seen there.

As for the later Coptic usage, it is not clear to me that the inscriptions originated in an attempt to rededicate the site so much as simply to use it. The hieroglyphs and images of earlier gods are minimal in comparison to the Coptic inscriptions. Furthermore, while one figure has been scratched out in the scene that includes the god Min with his erect phallus, it seems telling that Min is left unscathed in all his glory.[23] As for the boats, hunters, and animals, they hardly seem offensive in and of themselves. Monks after all

21. Meyer, "Archeological Survey," 81–82.

22. The date of the various elements might well vary. The evidence of quarrying seems limited, though further exploration could clarify this. In addition, the Byzantine shards scattered about the obelisk site makes one wonder about the connection. Might it have been a stopping point on the way to the overhang?

23. While the hieroglyph for the plural of "gods" does appear (Meyer, "Archaeological Survey," 81; Meyer, "Wadi Sheiklh Ali Survey," 23), it seems unlikely that later era Coptic monks would have known it.

experienced the same world as those around them with its hunters, animals, and boats. Animals often figure in monastic stories, and at least the larger monasteries had their own boats that plied the Nile.[24] While the boats depicted on the cliffs may not have corresponded with those belonging to the monasteries,[25] one imagines that the etchings seemed relatively harmless to the monks.

The Coptic inscriptions, on the other hand, offer clear evidence of the site's religious significance to those who visited it. Pious requests to be remembered, to be remembered in prayer, to be granted mercy, and the like abound. Whether the requests, in general, were directed to the Lord, a saint associated with or perhaps even buried at the site, or simply to monks who might later visit and use the site remains unclear. That it was visited regularly and repeatedly by some monks is certain. If the overhang served as a retreat from the valley, a place of deep withdrawal into the desert, perhaps from a communal monastery,[26] its remoteness meant that the withdrawn monk(s) could not have stayed long without the delivery of additional supplies of food and water. It would only be natural in the course of such sojourns that individual monks might have noticed and scratched out an occasional offending image, though the evidence for it remains uneven at best. As such, it seems secondary to what originally drew the Coptic visitors to the site.

As for the possibility that visitation arose due to the site's association with a revered figure or saint, either through his earlier use of the site or his burial there, as Meyer notes, no evidence exists that either supports or eliminates the possibility. It is interesting note, however, that the Pachomian vita tradition preserves evidence of concern over the memorializing of a famous figure after his death at the site of his burial. In the Bohairic *Life of Pachomius*,

24. Goehring, "The Ship of the Pachomian Federation: Metaphor and Meaning in a Late Account of PachomianMonasticism," 289–303.

25. The boats depicted with the figures at the back recall images in pharaonic reliefs.

26. Shenoute withdrew to a cave some distance from the White Monastery, though not nearly so distant as the Wadi Sheikh Ali site is from any know habitation.

as Pachomius nears death, he repeatedly asks Theodore to remove his body from the place where it will be buried. The passage reads:

> Then he turned to Theodore and spoke to him, 'If the Lord visits me, do not leave my body in the place it will be buried in.' Grief-stricken, he answered him, 'I will do what you say.' Then he grabbed his beard, struck him on the breast, and said a second time, 'Theodore, pay atten- tion. Do not leave my body in the place where it will be buried.' Again he answered him, 'My Lord and father, I will do gratefully whatever you command me.' Theodore thought to himself that he was saying this so insistently out of fear some people would steal his body and build a *martyrion* for it as they do for the holy martyrs. For many times he had heard him criticize those who did such things, <saying, 'The saints have not been pleased with those who do such things,> because everyone who does this is commercializing the bodies of the saints. Then he seized him again by the beard and said to him a third time, 'Theodore, take care to do quickly what I have told you.'[27]

The following section recounts Pachomius's death and his burial by the brothers on the mountain (the monastic cemetery), after which they return to the monastery. Later, Theodore returns to honor Pachomius' earlier request.

> After they had come down from the mountain, Theodore that night took three other brothers with him, removed him from the place he had been buried, and put him with Apa Paphnouti, the brother of Apa Theodore and

27. Bohairic *Life of Saint Pachomius* (*SBo*) 122; translation by Armand Veil- leux, 177. The First Greek *Life of Pachomius* (*G1*) 116 has a much condensed version: "And he was in pain, at the point of giving up his spirit. He grabbed Theodore by the beard and said to him, 'If they hide my bones take them away from there.' Theodore thought he was enjoining him not to leave his body in the place of its burial but to transfer it elsewhere secretly. So [Pachomius] told him, 'I say not only this to you but also this.' And he enjoined him three times." Veilleuix, *Pachomian Koinonia*, 1.179.

accountant of the *Koinonia. No one knows to this day
where he lies.* (Deut. 34:6)[28]

While the triple repetition of Pachomius' request and the notion of commercializing the bodies of the saints reflect the hand
of the later author, the inclusion of the episode underscores an
awareness of the debate over relics and their commemoration in
the period of the text's production. Whether it represents an historical event, namely, the removal of Pachomius' body to a secret
location to avoid his grave becoming a pilgrimage site, or a literary
device designed to underscore monastic humility, the story indicates an awareness of such sites in Upper Egypt in the period in
question. I do not mean to suggest here that the Wadi Sheikh Ali
site served as the final resting place of Pachomius, though I sup-
pose that remains a possibility, but only that its possible function
as a pilgrimage site where local monks paid homage to a revered
saint finds support in the sources. The recent recovery of what appears to be the site of Shenoute's burial within the White Monastery complex serves as a case in point. It represents the emerging
reality of the veneration of the saints against which the Pachomian
episode offered a counterpoise of ascetic humility.

In closing, let me repeat that the process of writing this essay has been a journey that mingled happy memories of my past
adventures with Marv with a present sadness at his loss. While our
early plans of returning to the site for fuller documentation and
eventual publication never materialized, I hope that the present
essay with its pictures might renew scholarly interest in it.[29] Finally,
I had hoped that the slides from the Wadi Sheikh Ali had included
a good photo of Marv to use in this account. Unfortunately, my
focus on the site and its inscriptions proved detrimental in this
regard. I could not then have imagined my current need. I close
therefore with a photograph of Marv taken two days earlier in our
survey of the nearby village of al-Qasr. Surrounded by local vil-

28. *SBo* 123; translation from Veilleux, *Pachomian Koinonia* 179; *G1* does
not contain this account.

29. I plan eventually to digitize my photographs and survey notes of the
Wadi Sheikh Ali, and make them available online.

lagers with his ruler, pencil, and survey sheet in hand, the picture captures Marv at work, the thoughtful, adventurous, and playful soul I knew and miss. Rest in peace, my friend.

Marv in al Qasr

Bibliography

Abd al-Masîh, Yassa, Walter C. Till, and O. H. E. Khs-Burmester. "Coptic Graffiti and Inscriptions from the Monastery of Phoebammon." In *Le monastère de Phoebammon dans la Thébaide*, edited by Roger Rémondon et al., vol. 2, 21–102, and plates iii–v. Cairo: Société d'Archéologie Copte, 1965.

Beebe, H. Keith, and Marvin W. Meyer, "Literary and Archaeological Survey of al-Qasr." *Newsletter of the American Research Center in Egypt* 121 (1983) 25–31 + 2 plates.

Crum, W. E., and H. G. Evelyn-White. *The Monastery of Epiphanius at Thebes.* 2 vols. 1926. Reprinted, Milan: Cisalpino–La Goliardica, 1977.

Goehring, James E. *Ascetics, Society, and The desert: Studies in Early Egyptian Monasticism.* Harrisburg, PA: Trinity, 1999.

———. "Sheikh Ali, Wadi." In *Encyclopedia of Early Christian Art and Archeology.* Edited by Paul Corby Finney. New York: Garland, forthcoming.

————. "The Ship of the Pachomian Federation: Metaphor and Meaning in a Late Account of PachomianMonasticism." In *Christianity in Egypt: Literary Production and Intellectual Trends*, edited by Paolo Buzi and Alberto Camplani, 289–303. SEA 125. Rome: Instituto Patristico Augustinianum, 2011.

Layton, Bentley. *A Coptic Grammar: With Chrestomathy and Glossary: Sahidic Dialect*. Porta linguarum orientalium n.s. 20. Wiesbaden: Harrassowitz, 2000.

Meyer, Marvin W. "Archaeological Survey of the Wadi Sheikh Ali: December 1980." *Göttingen Miszellen* 64 (1983) 77–82.

————. "Wadi Sheikh Ali." *The Coptic Encyclopedia*, edited by Aziz Suryal Atiya, 7:2312a–13a. New York: Macmillan, 1991. http://ccdl.libraries.claremont.edu/cdm/ref/collection/cce/id/1906.

————. "Wadi Sheikh Ali Survey, December 1980." *Newsletter of the American Research Center in Egypt* 117 (1982) 22–24.

Rémondon, Roger. "Graffiti Grecs du Monastère de Phoebammon." In *Le Monastère de Phoebammon dans la Thébaïde*, edited by Charles Bachatly, vol. 2, 1–20 and plates i–ii. Cairo: La Société d'Archéologie Copte, 1965.

Veilleuix, Armand, trans. *Pachomian Koinonia*. Kalamazoo, MI: Cistercian Publications, 1980.

7

Salome and Jesus at the Table
in the Gospel of Thomas[1]

Kathleen E. Corley

FOR AT LEAST A decade, scholars have discussed the characteristic
presence of women in the Jesus Movements and Christian Gnostic
groups. Several sayings of the *Gospel of Thomas,* more notably
Saying 114, have led scholars to posit the presence of women in
the Thomas community.[2] This is not surprising, given Thomas's
Syrian provenance and ascetic outlook, as Syrian Christianity
generally was characterized by a radical asceticism in which both
women and men participated.[3] Another saying in the *Gospel
of Thomas,* however, may further inform our understanding of
women in the Thomas community, Syrian Christianity, and ascetic
Christian groups: Saying 61, from which one may infer that Jesus
is reclining on a dining couch with the woman disciple, Salome.
This saying betrays controversy in the Thomas community over
whether or not the salvation of women by means of "becoming
male" should be taken to the extreme of allowing them to recline

1. Reprinted with permission from SBL Press. This article originally appeared in *Semeia* 86 (1999).

2. King, "The Kingdom," 66; Kloppenborg et al., *Q–Thomas Reader,* 111–
12; Valantasis, *The Gospel of Thomas,* 194–195.

3. Brock and Harvey, *Holy Women of the Syrian Orient*; Harvey, "Women
in Early Syrian Christianity."

like men at community meals, becoming part of a kind of "masculine fellowship."[4] This places the Thomas community squarely within its Hellenistic milieu, both in its gender inclusivity and in its ambiguity over the consequences that such an egalitarian ethic might entail. The appearance of women at communal meals is characteristic of Greco-Roman times. That means that gender-inclusive meals, although noteworthy, were not unique in the social world of the *Gospel of Thomas*. I have suggested that such gender inclusive meals, which were characteristic of Christian groups generally, show that early Christians were participants in the innovative culture of their times. Thus, gender-inclusive meals were not distinctively Christian, but were rather the result of an Empire-wide social innovation beginning in the Late Republican era, whereby women began having increased access to the "public" sphere of men, and began attending public meals. This innovation in the meal practices of Greco-Roman women was met with strong resistance, as it undermined the social and gender based hierarchy of Greco-Roman society. As such behavior had long been associated with the less restricted behavior of lower class women, slave women, prostitutes, and courtesans, women who ventured out in public in this manner or attended public meals with men were labeled "slaves," "courtesans," or "prostitutes," regardless of their actual social status, occupation, or social position. This fluctuation in Greco-Roman meal etiquette may be found throughout the Hellenized Mediterranean world, even in Palestine.[5]

Thus, it is notable that the *Gospel of Thomas* reflects this fluctuation in Greco-Roman table etiquette. In particular, Thomas is the only gospel in which Jesus is clearly described as dining with a woman in the modern Roman manner, as he dines with her on the same couch. In other gospel traditions, women merely remain seated or kneeling at Jesus' feet (Matt 26:6–13; Mark 14:3–9; Luke 7:36–50; 10:38–42; John 12:2–8). As Sterling Bjorndahl first pointed out, this is a very scandalous image indeed, as it would imply

4. Here I use the phrase coined by Attridge.

5. Corley, "Were the Women around Jesus Really Prostitutes?"; Corley, *Private Women, Public Meals.*

a close, even sexual relationship between Jesus and Salome, given the meal context of the scene (Appendix). The meal context of the Saying probably contributed to the myriad of textual corruptions found throughout, as translators and scribes no doubt found the sexualized scene troubling.

Saying 61a opens with a saying of Jesus known from the Synoptic tradition: "Two will rest on a couch; one will die, one will live." The Coptic word should here be taken in the sense of the Greek word koité, which maybe rendered "bed," but also "couch" or "dining couch," as a meal setting is implied by Salome's response in 61b.[6] Notably, the apocalyptic implications of being taken away to judgment found in Luke 17:34 are absent here. *Gos. Thom.* 61a is rather a wisdom saying about the random nature of death which has secondarily been given a Gnostic interpretation in this context.[7] Here, issues of "life" and "death" are to be decided on the basis of whether one is "undivided" and "filled with light" like Jesus, rather than being "divided" and "filled with darkness" (Saying 61e, f). However, between the statement that "one will die and one will live" and the Gnostic soteriological comments about "light" and being "whole" or "undivided," is placed a dialogue between Jesus and Salome.

Salome in Early Christian Tradition

Salome is a well-known figure in early Christian literature, and is the second most frequently mentioned female disciple of Jesus next to Mary Magdalene. In canonical traditions, she is mentioned by name only in Mark, who names her with the other women who were present at the crucifixion (Mark 15:40) and at the empty tomb (Mark 16:1). By inference from the other gospel accounts, Salome has also at times been identified with the mother of the sons of Zebedee (Matt 27–56) and with the sister of Mary the

---

6. That the "couch" in question in *Gos. Thom.* 61 is a dining couch has been noticed for some time; Bjorndahl, "Thomas 61–78," 9 n. 17; Layton, *Gnostic Scriptures*, 391, n. f; Meyer, *Gospel of Thomas*, 47, 93.

7. Patterson, *Gospel of Thomas and Jesus*, 47.

mother of Jesus, who is sometimes called Mary Clopas (John
19:25), hence she is often referred to in early Christian literature as
"Mary Salome." Like Mary Magdalene, Salome is also mentioned
in other apocryphal texts besides the *Gospel of Thomas*. In the
Secret Gospel of Mark, Salome, along with Jesus' mother Mary, is
denied an audience with Jesus (2r:16). She appears in other dialogues with Jesus, such as the *Pistis Sophia* (1.54, 58; 3.132) as well
as in the Syriac *Testament of Our Lord* (1:15–16). Almost all of
Clement of Alexandria's quotations of the *Gospel of the Egyptians*
are dialogues between Jesus and Salome, many of which contain
parallels to sayings of Jesus found in the *Gospel of Thomas (Misc,
iii. 45, 64, 66, 68, 91f., 97; Excerpta ex Theodoti* 67). She also occurs
in a list of female disciples in the *First Apocalypse of James* (40,
9–26). Furthermore, Salome is also one of Jesus' disciples in various Manichaean Psalms, most notably in a "Q-like" description of
the sending of the disciples to wander and preach. In this psalm,
Jesus chooses several disciples to be missionaries, most of whom
are men, to go from village to village, walk along the roads, take
no food or drink, etc. However, he also sends out several women,
among them Salome and Mary (presumably) Magdalene.[8] In another Manichaean Psalm, Salome seems to serve an almost priestly
function, and "builds a tower upon a rock" rather than Peter.[9]
Finally, as is the case with many popular disciple figures, apocryphal legends became associated with Salome, particularly stories
connecting her to the infancy narratives as a midwife, which were
later conflated with stories about a reformed whore.[10]

Notably, many of the references to Salome in early Christian literature besides the *Gospel of Thomas* have Syrian roots,
particularly the *First Apocalypse of James,* the Syriac *Testament of
our Lord,* and the Manichaean Psalms. In fact, a recent article by
Richard Bauckham accounts for the appearance of Salome in the
Gospel of Thomas on the basis of an East Syrian strand of tradition

8. Allberry, *Manichaean Psalm Book,* 192:21ff; 194:19–22.
9. Ibid., 222:1–3.
10. Corley, "Salome."

independent of the Gospel of Mark.[11] It is notable that in the Manichaean Psalms we find Salome and other women described as being sent out in a group of wandering, ascetic itinerants, which is precisely the kind of community now envisioned in the Syrian community which produced the *Gospel of Thomas*.[12] Bauckham also considers the mention of Salome in the Manichaean Psalms to be of East Syrian provenance.[13] In this respect, the *Gospel of Thomas* is also seen to be in line with the Q tradition, which also reflects a similar tradition of wandering charismatics.[14] This suggests that the appearance of Salome on the couch with Jesus in the *Gospel of Thomas* reflects the participation of women in Syrian Christian groups which practiced asceticism.

However, Saying 61 in Thomas can also be shown to reflect a struggle over Salome's status, more akin to that found in the *Secret Gospel of Mark*. The rejection of Salome in *Secret Mark* has often been explained as a polemic against Salome due to her popularity with heretical Christian groups.[15] In Thomas, discomfort with Salome's presence at the table with Jesus can be seen in the placement of the dialogue between Jesus and Salome after the declaration that "two are on a couch, one will live and one will die." As Jesus and Salome are the "two on the couch," given that Jesus is the one who is "whole" and "undivided," by implication, Salome is the one who will die.[16] This implies both a criticism of Salome, and furthermore puts her soteriological status in question.

However, in Thomas, the meal setting alone may account for this discomfort with her proximity to Jesus, as the opening saying about "two on a couch" implies that Jesus and Salome are on

11. Bauckham, "Salome," 259.

12. Cameron, "Gospel of Thomas," 535–36; Meyer, *The Gospel of Thomas,* 9–10; Valantasis, *Gospel of Thomas*, 139.

13. Bauckham, "Salome," 263; Allberry, *Manichaean Psalm Book*, xix

14. Patterson, *The Gospel of Thomas*; Cameron, "Gospel of Thomas"; Robinson, "From Q to Thomas," 137–42.

15. M. Smith, *Clement of Alexandria*, 189–92; Levin, "Early History of Christianity," 4287.

16. Bjorndahl, "Thomas 61–78," 13.

the couch together, and not seated separately. Given the ascetic nature of the Thomas community, such a situation might have been construed as overly sexual, given the stereotypically sexualized nature of banquet scenes. Although certain monastic groups were among those philosophical and religious groups that held communal meals with both men and women during this time of social change, in deference to Hellenistic moral scruples, men and women monastics usually reclined at separate tables.[17] Rather than reflecting some sort of "bridal chamber" ritual,[18] Gos. Thom. 61 probably reflects the growing Hellenistic practice of including women in ancient communal meals. In addition, it reflects discomfort with a more liberal version of this practice, by having the woman join the man on the same couch, as if she were some sort of courtesan of Greek fame, or a socially progressive Roman matron. Saying 61 can thus be compared to Saying 114, in that the presence of a woman among the disciples is questioned, and then defended. However, in this instance the criticism of the woman does not come from the direction of the opposition, as in the case of Peter's attack on Mary in 114, but directly from Jesus. Poor Salome is left to defend herself. Salome's response is thus somewhat contentious, and rightly so: "Who are you, mister? You have climbed onto my couch and have eaten from my table like a stranger," which asserts that Jesus is the one responsible for the situation, not Salome.

In light of the controversial meal context implied in the saying, Layton's emendation, "as if you were someone special" or "as if you are from someone" as a possible mistranslation of the Greek should be carefully reconsidered.[19] Although the term xenos can

17. The Theraputae described by Philo arc a case in point. See Corley, 1989:66–75; Kraemer, "Monastic Jewish Women in Graeco-Roman Egypt." It may well be that the Essene meals included women as well. See Meeks, "Image of the Androgyne," 178–79 n. 70.

18. Buckley, "An Interpretation of Logion 114"; Buckley, Female Fault and Fulfillment.

19. The text or translation is corrupt at this point. Many translators and inlerpreters, however, have followed a rendering possible without emendation suggested by Attridge, "Greek Equivalents of Two Coptic Phrases," 32. See Bjorndahl, "Thomas 61–78," 9, 13; Meyer, Gospel of Thomas, 93. Bentley

indeed mean "stranger" or "foreigner" in the sense of Christians or Gnostics being estranged from the world, travelers or "passers-by" on the earth,[20] given that such notions have now been linked to the wandering ascetic lifestyle of the Thomas community),[21] it could also be rendered in this context "guest," or even "friend," as in one receiving hospitality, or being admitted to table fellowship.[22] This would link Saying 61 to an itinerant practice among Syrian Christians who would travel from village to village, and eat in the homes of others "like strangers."[23] In the context of Saying 61, however, Salome is cast in the role of the host, welcoming Jesus as the ἕνος (Matt 25:35–44). In this regard, *Gos. Thom.* 61 is in many ways similar to Luke 10,which is also best understood in the context of early Christian itinerancy where Jesus is greeted and served by Martha and joined at the table by Mary.[24] Here, however, Salome's role is similar to that of Martha, who in Luke 10 is pictured as the host of the house, and is discouraged. However, Salome's role as Jesus' disciple differs from that played by Mary in Luke 10, in that there, Mary takes the more conservative meal posture of a respectable wife, as she sits at Jesus' feet, and does not recline with him at the table.[25] Luke also clearly discourages women from joining the ranks of male itinerants, by including "wives" among those things that the men leave behind when they go out to preach.[26] In contrast, in *Gos. Thom.* 61, Salome is by implication reclining

---

Layton, however, tentatively translates this "like a stranger"(*Gnostic Scriptures*, 391), and notes the possible readings in his critical notes (*Nag Hammadi Codex II, 2–7,* 74). See now also Valantasis, *Gospel of Thomas*, 138–39.

20. For the connotations of "stranger" in Syrian asceticism, see Brock, "Early Syrian Asceticism," 9; Kraemer, "Conversion of Women," 301.

21. Patterson, *The Gospel of Thomas*; Meyer, *The Gospel of Thomas,* 11; Valantasis, *Gospel of Thomas*, 139.

22. LSJ; Stählin.

23. See also the *Didache* 11, 2 and 4; 2 John 5ff., which discuss hospitality being extended to wandering prophets, apostles, missionaries, and preachers (Stählin: 22–23).

24. Corley, *Private* Women, 133–44.

25. Ibid.

26. Ibid., 115; Schüssler Fiorenza, *In Memory of Her*, 145.

with Jesus for the meal, and asserts her discipleship in a clear and unambiguous way, claiming Jesus' own behavior as the source for the practice.[27] Thus, this saying implies the practice of wandering itinerancy now thought characteristic of the Thomas community, but furthermore reflects controversy over the presence of women in that community. More specifically, Saying 61 also implies a common Hellenistic struggle over the presence of women at meals with men.

As well as implying criticism of Salome, Saying 61 in its final form also serves to defend her, in that she declares herself a "disciple" of Jesus. This statement follows quickly upon Jesus' reply to her stinging retort, "Who are you, mister?" In his reply, Jesus makes a comment about his origin and nature. He is the one who "comes from that which is 'undivided' or 'whole' and who was "given things belonging to his Father." Following Salome's declaration of discipleship, Jesus reinforces the notion that to be like him, one must be "undivided" in order to be "filled with light". Thus, by claiming to be Jesus' disciple, Salome is claiming that she too is "undivided" or "whole" and "filled with light."

Although the concept of "light" is an important one in the *Gospel of Thomas,* particularly in the context of Gnostic ideas about the divine spark which enlightens the Gnostic believer,[28] for the purpose of time, I would like to focus on Salome's insistence that she is a disciple in that she is "undivided" or "whole," as it is this characteristic which has implications for her being a member of the "in-group" of Jesus' disciples as a woman and therefore present at a meal with Jesus.

In the context of Christian Gnostic soteriology, it is now generally recognized that the notion of being "undivided" or "whole" reflects a return to a primordial unity. The first human (Adam) was neither male nor female, but was rather androgynous.[29] Humanity

27. Valantasis, *Gospel of Thomas,* 139.

28. Sayings 24, 83; Bjorndahl, "Thomas 61–78," 14; Meyer, *Gospel of Thomas,* 80–81.

29. Sayings 4, 11, 16, 22, 23, 49, 75, 106; Bjorndahl, "Thomas 61–78," 14–15; Cameron, "Gospel of Thomas," 539; King, "The Kingdom," 66 n. 35; Klijn,

was then secondarily "divided" into male and female, this division being the reason for the current human condition. In the process of Gnostic salvation, then, one returns to this primordial state, being neither male nor female. In the *Gospel of Thomas*, the notion of being "undivided" or somehow reintegrated[30] is therefore related to being made a "single one" or even becoming a "solitary".[31] Other ancient texts have been used to link such ideas in *Thomas* to a practice of rigorous asceticism.[32] Thus, in *Thomas*, the ideal being "undivided," "whole," or "integrated" in Saying 61 coheres with *Thomas'* general proclivity for following an ascetic lifestyle, which would include, although not be limited to, abstention from sexual relations.[33]

However, the primordial unity held up as an ideal was also imagined to be a *male* androgyne.[34] Furthermore, definitions of ascetic spirituality assumed the superiority of characteristics defined as "masculine," such as reason, mind, and "spiritual courage" whereas characteristics defined as "feminine," such as emotion, bodily desire, and sexuality were to be denied.[35] Hence, in many early Christian traditions which emulated the ascetic life, Gnostic or otherwise, we find such epithets as "flee femininity" and "destroy the works of femaleness".[36] Thus, in the context of Gnostic and ascetic discourse, notions of the development of a higher

---

"The 'Single One' in the Gospel of Thomas"; Meeks, "Image of the Androgyne"; Meyer, "Making Mary Male."

30. Layton, *Gnostic Scriptures*, 391.

31. Cameron, "Gospel of Thomas," 539, 1986; Meyer, "Making Mary Male"; Valantasis, *Gospel of Thomas*, 195.

32. A point commonly made. See King, "The Kingdom," 69–70. See parallel language in *Gos. Eg.* 5; 2 *Clem* 12.:2–6; Baarda; Callan.

33. Bjorndahl, "Thomas 61–78," 15–20.

34. As in Philo's ideal of a male androgyne. See Attridge, "Masculine Fellowship," 410; King, "The Kingdom," 66 n. 35; Klijn, "'Single One,'" 276–78. On the original androgyne in Philo, see Baer, *Philo's Use*. For the significance of Philo's language for Gnostic sources, see Baer, *Philo's Use*, 72–74.

35. Castelli, "Virginity and Its Meaning"; Seim, "Ascetic Autonomy?"

36. Castelli, "Virginity and Its Meaning," 74–75; Seim, "Ascetic Autonomy?," 136; Wisse, "Flee Femininity."

spirituality as well as a return to a primordial unity coincide with notions of "becoming male." The process of Gnostic salvation is therefore a kind of "masculinization."[37] Thus, Salome's claim to "undivided" status or "wholeness" should also be seen in the same light as Mary's claim to "maleness" in Saying 114.[38] Given the Syrian provenance of the *Gospel of Thomas*, it is significant that in the context of Syrian Christianity, women ascetics were also characteristically described as "becoming like men."[39]

However, although it is true that in some sense Gnostics or others taking on the ascetic life—both males and females—would be called upon to denigrate "femininity" by achieving "maleness", [40] it is not the case that such an image can be interpreted to mean the same thing when used of women. Elizabeth Castelli has shown that such symbolic categories have a very different meaning for women's spirituality, in that women, unlike men, are required to negate their own femininity in order to achieve this higher spiritual status. In fact, women ascetics are described as acting out "being men" by cross-dressing, and may have interpreted changes in their physical bodies brought on by rigorous ascetic practices (lack of menses, etc.) to be a sign of their elevated spirituality.[41] The

37. So Filoramo, *History of Gnosticism*, 177: "The process of salvation, in this sense is essentially male; a process, as it were, of masculinization. The final equilibrium re-established in the bosom of the archetypal Androgyne will therefore be an equilibrium in which the male is destined to triumph." See Clement of Alexandria, *Excerpta ex Theodoti* 79; *1 Apoc. Jas.* 41, 15–19; *Zost.* 131, 2–10.

38. Here I am consciously in disagreement with Meyer, who considers imagery in Saying 22 to be separate from that of 114 ("Making Mary Male"; *Gospel of Thomas*, 110) as well as with Wisse, who is against interpreting 114, 22 and 61 in light of each other (305). Sec also Bjorndahl, "Thomas 61–78," 14–15; Perkins, *Gnosticism and the New Testament*, 70–71.

39 As were many ancient ascetic women. See Castelli, "Virginity and Its Meaning," 74–77; on Syrian Christian women, see Harvey, "Women in Early Syrian Christianity," 297. See also Lagrand.

40. Arai, "To Make Her Male," 375; Meyer, "Making Mary Male," 567; Kloppenborg et al., *Q–Thomas Reader*, 111–12.

41. Castelli, "Virginity and Its Meaning," 74–77; Clark, "Women and Asceticism," 39; King, "The Kingdom," 66 n. 36; Seim, "Ascetic Autonomy?", 135.

practice of asceticism thus had denigrating practical consequences for ancient women, in spite of the greater social mobility it may have provided.[42]

However, it is significant that "becoming male" may have had practical consequences in the activities of ascetic women, as this may shed light on Salome's defense of her discipleship and presence with Jesus on the banquet couch by means of her "undivided" and fully integrated male status. Ron Cameron has recently suggested that a major social setting of the Thomas community was that of community meals or "table fellowship".[43] Inclusion in these meals would have been central to the self-identity of the group.[44] Baptism was the rite of initiation into the Thomas community, as it was the symbol of having become a "solitary" or a "single one".[45] Baptism could serve this symbolic function, as it symbolized the reunification of the sexes and the return to a primordial unity.[46],[47] One could therefore argue that Saying 61 reflects an interpretation of community inclusion which admitted women to the table fellowship of the *Thomas* community by virtue of their having achieved this unified male state though baptism.[48] Saying 61 in the *Gospel of Thomas* would therefore place the Thomas community well within the context of other Syrian Christian groups who practiced a radical sexual asceticism in order to achieve liberation

42. Castelli, "Virginity and Its Meaning"; Clark, "Women and Asceticism," 38; Harvey, "Women in Early Syrian Christianity," 295–96; against Burrus, *Chastity as Autonomy*.

43. Cameron, "Gospel of Thomas," 539.

44. Ibid.; Crossan, *Four Other Gospels*, 51–52; King, "The Kingdom," 70.

45. Cameron, "Gospel of Thomas," 539; King, "The Kingdom," 68.

46. Attridge, "Masculine Fellowship," 410–11; Cameron, "Gospel of Thomas," 539; Meeks, "Image of the Androgyne," 185.

47. For the significant discussion of the significance of baptism in *Thomas,* see J. Z. Smith, "Garments of Shame." Smith has recently been rebutted by De Conick and Fossum who argue that *Gos. Thom,* 37 docs not reflect a baptismal practice, but rather an unction ceremony.

48. So Attridge, who links the rite of baptism, the myth of primordial unity, and the goal of becoming "male" ("Masculine Fellowship," 410). See now Valantasis, *Gospel of Thomas,* 139.

from "femininity," joining a "masculine fellowship," literally, a "brotherhood" by virtue of their baptismal initiation.[49] One of the consequences of baptism in the *Gospel of Thomas*; however, could be the inclusion of women in communal meals usually limited to men. Given this demonstrated relationship between Sayings 61 and 114, Saying 114 may not be simply challenging Mary's general presence among the circle of disciples, but may rather imply a challenge to her being present with the men for community meals, as it is presence at community meals, as well as baptism, which marks one's membership in the group.[50] Jesus affirms that Mary may be present if she too is "made male." Salome's dinner with Jesus in the *Gospel of Thomas* can thus be shown to shed light on Thomas and the community which produced it in several ways. First, it reflects Thomas' Syrian provenance, in that other Syrian Christian groups included both men and women—men and women who renounced their sexuality and practiced an ascetic lifestyle. In doing so, they may have interpreted their asceticism as reflecting their return to a primordial unity or wholeness that was "neither male nor female," and yet was a condition still essentially male according to ancient symbolic categories. Moreover, other Syrian women ascetic characters besides Mary and Salome could be described as "becoming like men." Thus, as is the case with Saying 114, Saying 61 can be shown to reflect controversy over using such symbolic categories to allow for the presence of women in the Thomas community. However, given the implicit criticism of Salome's presence on a dining couch with Jesus, Saying 61 may also reflect controversy over the presence of women in the communal meals of the group. Second, Saying 61 also reflects the lifestyle of itinerancy now imagined for the Thomas community, in that Salome is pictured as hosting a meal for Jesus as a "guest" or "stranger." This further serves to connect the *Gospel of Thomas*

49. "Attridge, "Masculine Fellowship."

50. Cameron, "The Gospel of Thomas," 539. The possibility of these two named women being "Mary Salome" should thus be reconsidered, as it is not clear that the "Mary" of 114 is Magdalene (Kloppenborg, *Q–Thomas Reader*, 112).

to Q, in that Q also reflects a lifestyle of radical itinerancy,[51] and, as I have argued elsewhere, the presence of women at communal meals.[52] Finally, these observations further call into question the ways in which the *Gospel of Thomas* may be called "Gnostic," in that Saying 61 reflects ideas and practices common to a Hellenistic milieu more generally, and to Syrian Christianity and early Christian asceticism more specifically.[53]

Bibliography

Allberry, C. R. C. *A Manichaean Psalmbook, Part* 2. Stuttgart: Kohlhammer, 1938.

Arai, Sasagu. "To Make Her Male: An Interpretation of Logion 114 in the Gospel of Thomas." *Studia Patristica* 24 (1993) 371–76.

Attridge, Harold W. "Greek Equivalents of Two Coptic Phrases: CG I, 1.65, 9–10 and CG II, 2.43.26." *Bulletin of the American Society of Papyrologists* 18 (1981) 27–32.

———. "Masculine Fellowship in the *Acts of Thomas*." *The Future of Early Christianity: Essays in Honor of Helmut Koester,* edited by Birger Pearson, 406–13. Minneapolis: Fortress, 1991

Baarda. T. "2 Clement 12 and the Sayings of Jesus." In *Early Transmission of the Words of Jesus: Thomas, Tatian, and the Text of the New Testament: A Collection of Studies,* edited by J. Helderman and S. J. Noorda, 261–88. Amsterdam: VU Boekhandel, 1983.

Baer, Richard A. *Philo's Use of the Categories Male and Female.* Arbeiten zur Literatur und Geschichte des hellenistischen Judentums 3. Leiden: Brill, 1970.

Bauckham, Richard. "Salome the Sister of Jesus, Salome the Disciple of Jesus, and the Secret Gospel of Mark." *Novum Testamentum* 33 (1991) 245–75.

Bjorndahl, Sterling. "Thomas 61–78: A Chreia Elaboration." Major paper, The Claremont Graduate School, 1988.

Brock, S. P. "Early Syrian Asceticism." *Numen* 20 (1973) 1–19.

Brock, Sebastian, and Susan Harvey. *Holy Women of the Syrian Orient.* Transformation of the Classical Heritage 13. Berkeley: University of California Press, 1987.

Buckley, Jorunn Jacobsen. "An Interpretation of Logion 114 in the Gospel of Thomas." *Novum Testamentum* 27 (1985) 243–72.

51. Cameron, "Gospel of Thomas"; Patterson, *Gospel of Thomas and Jesus*; Robinson, "From Q to the Gospel of Thomas."

52. Corley, "Women and Lament in Q."

53. Attridge, "Masculine Fellowship," 412–13.

————. *Female Fault and Fulfillment in Gnosticism.* Chapel Hill: University of North Carolina Press.

Burrus, Virginia. *Chastity as Autonomy: Women in the Stories of the Apocryphal Acts.* Lewiston, NY: Mellen, 1987.

Cameron, Ron. "Parable and Interpretation in the Gospel of Thomas." *Forum* 2.2 (1986) 3–39.

————. "The Gospel of Thomas and Christian Origins." In *The Future of Early Christianity: Essays* in *Honor of Helmut Koester,* edited by Birger Pearson, 381–92. Minneapolis: Fortress, 1991.

Castelli, Elizabeth. "Virginity and Its Meaning for Women's Sexuality in Early Christianity." *Feminist Studies of Religion* 2 (1986) 61–88.

Clark, Gillian. "Women and Asceticism in Late Antiquity: The Refusal of Status and Gender." In *Asceticism,* edited by Vincent L. Wimbush and Richard Valantasis, 33–48. Oxford: Oxford University Press, 1995.

Conick, April C. de, and Jarl Fossum. "Stripped Before God: A New Interpretation of Logia 37 in the Gospel of Thomas." *Vigiliae Christianae* 45 (1991) 123–50.

Corley, Kathleen E. "Salome." In *The International Standard Bible Encyclopedia,* edited by Geoffrey W. Bromiley, 4:286. Grand Rapids: Eerdmans, 1988.

————. "Were the Women around Jesus Really Prostitutes? Women in the Context of Greco-Roman Meals." *Society of Biblical Literature Seminar Papers* 28 (1989) 487–521.

————. *Private Women, Public Meals: Social Conflict in the Synoptic Tradition.* Peabody, MA: Hendrickson, 1993.

————. "Women, Gender and Lament in Q." In *Women and the Historical Jesus: Feminist Myths of Christian Origins,* 79–106. Minneapolis: Fortress, 2010.

Crossan, John Dominic. *Four Other Gospels: Shadows on the Contours of Canon.* 1985. Reprinted, Sonoma, CA: Polebridge, 1992.

Filoramo, Giovanni. *A History of Gnosticism.* Translated by Anthony Alcock. Oxford: Blackwell, 1990.

Harvey, Susan Ashbrook. "Women in Early Syrian Christianity." In *Images of Women in Antiquity,* edited by Averil Cameron and Amelie Kuhrt, 288–98. Detroit: Wayne State University Press, 1983.

Jefford, Clayton N. "The Dangers of Lying in Bed: Luke 17:34–35 and Parallels." *Forum* 5 (1990) 106–10.

King, Karen L. "The Kingdom in the Gospel of Thomas." *Forum* 3 (1987) 48–97.

Klijn, A. F. J. "The 'Single One' in the Gospel of Thomas." *Journal of Biblical Literature* 81 (1962) 271–78.

Kloppenborg, John et al. *Q–Thomas Reader.* Sonoma, CA: Polebridge, 1990.

Kraemer, Ross. "The Conversion of Women to Ascetic Forms of Christianity." *Signs* 6 (1980) 298–307.

————. "Monastic Jewish Women in Graeco-Roman Egypt: Philo Judaeus on the Therapeutrides." *Signs* 14 (1989) 342–70.

Lagrand, James. "How Was the Virgin Mary 'Like a Man'? A Note on Mt. 1:18b and Related Syriac Christian Texts." *Novum Testamentum* 22 (1980) 97–107.

Layton, Bentley. *The Gnostic Scriptures*. Garden City, NY: Doubleday, 1987.

————, ed. *Nag Hammadi Codex JI*, 2–7. Vol. 1. Leiden: Brill, 1989.

Levin, Saul. "The Early History of Christianity in Light of the 'Secret Gospel' of Mark." *Aufstieg und Niedergang der römischen Welt* 11.25: 4270–92. Berlin: de Gruyter, 1988.

Meeks, Wayne A. "The Image of the Androgyne: Some Uses of a Symbol in Earliest Christianity." *History of Religions* 13 (1974) 165–208.

Meyer, Marvin. "Making Mary Male in the Gospel of Thomas." In *New Testament Studies* 31 (1985) 554–70.

————. *The Gospel of Thomas: The Hidden Sayings of Jesus*. San Francisco: HarperSanFrancisco, 1992.

Patterson, Steve. *The Gospel of Thomas and Jesus*. Sonoma, CA: Polebridge, 1993.

Perkins, Pheme. *Gnosticism and the New Testament*. Minneapolis: Fortress, 1993.

Robinson, James M. "On Bridging the Gulf From Q to the Gospel of Thomas (or Vice Versa)." In *Nag Hammadi, Gnosticism and Early Christianity*, edited by Charles W. Hedrick and Robert Hodgson, Jr., 127–75. 1986. Reprinted, Eugene, OR: Wipf & Stock, 2005.

Schüssler Fiorenza, Elisabeth. *In Memory of Her: A Feminist Theological Reconstruction of Christian Origins*. New York: Crossroad, 1983.

Seim, Turid Karlsen. "Ascetic Autonomy? New Perspectives on Single Women in the Early Church." *Studia Theologica* 43 (1989) 125–40.

Smith, Jonathan Z. "The Garments of Shame." *History of Religions* 5 (1965) 217–38.

Smith, Morton. *Clement of Alexandria and a Secret Gospel of Mark*. Cambridge: Harvard University Press, 1973.

Valantasis, Richard. *The Gospel of Thomas*. London: Routledge, 1997.

Wisse, Frederik. "Flee Femininity: Antifemininity in Gnostic Texts and the Question of Social Milieu." In *Images of the Feminine in Gnosticism*, edited by Karen L. King, 297–307. Minneapolis: Fortress, 1988.

8

Nascent Christianity in Edessa

Stephen J. Patterson

MARVIN MEYER WAS ONE of the great scholars of Gnosticism, Nag Hammadi, and what became one of the most important discoveries at Nag Hammadi, the Coptic *Gospel of Thomas*. Many years ago Marvin and I collaborated on a translation of the *Gospel of Thomas* for the Polebridge Press project, *The Complete Gospels*, a translation that has subsequently enjoyed a long life on the internet. It even made its way into A Course in Miracles, when Gary Renard used part of it in his book, *Your Immortal Reality*, claiming that it had been revealed to him in his living room by an angelic being named Pursah. Marvin got quite a kick out of that. Imagine, angels using our translation as a point of reference! We, of course, had our own uses for that translation, among them further exploration of the kind of Christianity that grew up in the ancient city of Edessa, where this gospel was originally composed (presumably in someone's living room, without angelic help). I am happy to be able to dedicate the following very mortal ideas about Edessene Christianity to Marvin's posthumous Festschrift.

What was Christianity like in Edessa in this early period? A generation ago, Bauer conjectured that it was originally a Marcionite form of Christianity that was planted there around the middle of the second century.[1] But Christian sources from the second cen-

1. W. Bauer, *Orthodoxy and Heresy in Earliest Christianity* (R. Kraft, et

tury, including the *Odes of Solomon*, Tatian's *Oration to the Greeks*, the remnants of Bardaisan's school, and the *Acts of Thomas*, reveal a more complex view. Far from Marcionite, most of this material can only be described as Jewish Christian. It is also profoundly influenced by Hellenistic thought—especially the anthropological and cosmological speculations of the Middle Platonists. As with other Jewish Platonists, like Philo of Alexandria, for example, the Christians of Edessa spent time pondering Genesis 1 and 2, and what it might mean to be created in the image of God. Their ethos was world-renouncing, but only sometimes "encratite," and never grounded in the anti-cosmic dualism more typical of Marcionite or Manichaean mythic schemes. Salvation, however, does come by enlightenment, where Christ plays the role of helper and revealer. There is little talk of Jesus' death, and the idea of atonement seldom appears. A brief overview of the main sources will better set the religious milieu within which the *Gospel of Thomas* was born, and to which it also contributed.

The Odes of Solomon

Among the earliest Christian traditions from eastern Syria are arguably the *Odes of Solomon*, written near the end of the first, or the beginning of the second, century CE.[2] They may be described as "Jewish Christian" insofar as their focus is on God, not Christ, who

---

al., trans. and ed.; Philadelphia: Fortress, 1971), 28–29.

2. On the critical issues relating to the *Odes of Solomon* and the relevant literature see J. H. Charlesworth, "The Odes of Solomon," in *idem*, ed., *The Old Testament Pseudepigrapha* (Garden City: Doubleday, 1985) II: 725–34. For the first century date of the *Odes* see esp. J. Rendel Harris and A. Mingana, *The Odes and Psalms of Solomon* (2 vols.; New York, Longmans, Green, 1916–1920) II: 69; and R. Bultmann, "Ein jüdisch-christliches Psalmbuch aus dem ersten Jahrhundert," *Monatsschrift für Pastoraltheologie* 7 (1910) 23–29. For a contrary view, see Drijvers, "Apocryphal Literature in the Cultural Milieu of Osrhoëne," 244–45. For their Edessene provenance, see J. de Zwaan, "The Edessene Origin of the Odes of Solomon," 285–302 in R. P. Casey, et al., eds., *Quantulacumque: Studies Presented to Kirsopp Lake* (London: Christophers, 1937); and A. Vööbus, *History of Asceticism in the Syrian Orient* (CSCO 14; Louvain: Secrétariat du CSCO, 1958) I:62–64.

appears only with great ambiguity in several odes, where he may be referred to as "the Lord."[3] The birth of "the Son" is recounted in one ode,[4] and in another the resurrection[5] and Christ's descent into hell.[6] In this hymn the cross is also mentioned,[7] but not in connection with the concept of sacrifice and atonement. Rather, the ode sings of God's Righteous One, who was persecuted and thought to be dead, but is still alive—a well-known motif in Jewish Wisdom theology.[8] In the *Odes* "the Lord" is one who brings wisdom, truth, light, and knowledge to those who would attend to these things. Revelation comes by the Word—the Man, the Son, the Messiah—who "was known before the foundations of the world, that he might give life to persons forever by the truth of his name."[9] Salvation comes as a gift ("grace")—the gift of knowledge from the "Father of Knowledge" and "Word of Knowledge,"[10] who "was zealous that those things should be known which through his grace have been given to us."[11] His knowledge comes as a stream of water, as from a "living spring" flowing from "the lips of the Lord."[12] The "elect" seek him and are instructed to walk in his ways.[13] "Walk in the knowledge of the Lord and you will know the grace of the Lord generously."[14] The Lord promises the elect: "I will enter into you and bring you forth from destruction, and make

3. On the ambiguity and identity of Christ and God expressed in the title "Lord," see Charlesworth, "Odes of Solomon," 729.

4. *Odes Sol* 19:6–11.

5. *Odes Sol* 42:6.

6. *Odes Sol* 42:11–20.

7. *Odes Sol* 42:2.

8. Cf. Wis 2–3; the ode is a good example of G. W. E. Nickelsburg's early Jewish "stories of persecution and vindication of the righteous" (*Resurrection, Immortality, and Eternal Life in Intertestamental Judaism* [HTS 26; Cambridge: Harvard, 1972]).

9. *Odes Sol* 41:11–15.

10. *Odes Sol* 7:6.

11. *Odes Sol* 6:6.

12. *Odes Sol* 30.

13. *Odes Sol* 33:13.

14. *Odes Sol* 23:4.

you wise in the ways of truth."[15] At times the elect are identified with the Lord: "Behold, the Lord is our mirror. Open (your) eyes and see them in him."[16]

Throughout the *Odes*, the dualities of light/darkness, truth/falsehood, and immortality/corruption serve to mark out a universe of good and evil. The good is associated with that which is "above," and several of the *Odes* sing of mystical experiences in which the believer travels the heavens viewing the mysteries of the transcendent world above.[17] The God one encounters in such experiences is constantly praised in the *Odes* as one who loves and is loved, who shows mercy, kindness, grace, who offers wisdom, truth and understanding, and protection from adversaries. The tone is intimate, sometimes erotic.[18] In one of the *Odes*, God, though masculine, is depicted as having female breasts.[19] In another, Christ is depicted in feminine terms, offering milk from her breasts to those who would attain perfection and incorruptibility.[20] Other *Odes* seem to reflect the point of view of a woman.[21] It may well be that this collection of early Christian hymnody developed in a setting in which men and women both participated in creating liturgical materials, reflecting experiences shared across gender lines. One calls to mind Jewish sectarians described in Philo's *De Vita Contemplativa*, whose periodic night-long celebrations ended with choirs of men and women merging to form a common chorus, both male and female, to sing hymns in praise to God.[22]

15. *Odes Sol* 33:8.
16. *Odes Sol* 13:1; cf. 3:7–8.
17. *Odes Sol* 11:10–19; 35:1–7; 36:1–8; 41:6.
18. E.g., *Odes Sol* 3:1–8.
19. *Odes Sol* 19:1–4.
20. *Odes Sol* 8:14.
21. E.g., *Odes Sol* 14, 16, and possibly 3.
22. *Vita Cont* 83–89.

Tatian

Perhaps the best-known figure of early Christianity east of the Euphrates is Tatian. Tatian was a native of "Assyria,"[23] who as a young man went west to study rhetoric and philosophy among the great scholars of Rome. While there he was converted to Christianity while by reading the LXX,[24] and eventually joined the circle of Justin Martyr.[25] After the death of Justin, Tatian seems to have gone his own way and returned to the east, probably around 172 C.E.[26] He is credited with having written much,[27] but only the fragmentary remains of his gospel harmony, the *Diatessaron*,[28] and a most remarkable tract, the *Oration to the Greeks*,[29] survive.

The most striking thing about the *Oration to the Greeks* is its ascription to a Christian writer. Indeed, were we not familiar with Tatian and his history, this would not be considered a Christian work at all, but a kind of classic text of Hellenistic Judaism. In it, Christ scarcely appears at all.[30] When, in the course of the essay, Tatian describes his own conversion experience, it is not recounted as coming to know about Christ, but as a discovery of the wisdom and insight of certain ancient "barbaric" writings,[31] by which he means, presumably, the Jewish scriptures. To the Greeks, he sings

23. So he describes himself in *Or ad Graec* 42, the term generally designates the region east of the Euphrates extending east to Parthia.

24. *Or ad Graec* 29.

25. Irenaeus, *Haer* 1.28.1; Eusebius, *Hist eccles* 4.29.3. Tatian mentions Justin with affection and admiration in his *Or ad Graec* 18.

26. Eusebius, *Chron* 12; Epiphanius, *Adv Haer* 1.3.46. Beyond this there are no clear dates associated with his life.

27. Eusebius, *Hist eccles* 4.29.7.

28. For the relevant fragments and *testimonia* see D. Wünsch, *TRE* 10:628–29.

29. M. Whattaker, *Oratio ad Graecos and Fragments* (Oxford: Clarendon 1982).

30. He is clearly referred to only in ch. 21, but may also be alluded to in chs. 6 and 13.

31. *Or ad Graec* 29.1.

the praises not of Jesus, but of Moses, whom he regards as the most ancient of all sages.[32]

As with the *Odes of Solomon*, the theology expressed in this tract has much affinity with Platonically-oriented Jewish Wisdom theology. God, the "foundation of the whole," created the universe by the power of the Logos, an extension of God, like unto a flame that is passed from a fire to a torch, of like nature and undiminished, and yet separate.[33] Tatian's anthropology shares with much of Hellenistic Judaism its interest in the two creation accounts in Gen 1:27 and 2:7. The Logos, he says, created the human as an "image of immortality", so that like God, he might also be immortal.[34] Later, he explains that at creation, human beings were endowed with two types of "spirits" one called "soul" which connects a person to the material world, and another, "greater than the soul," called "the image and likeness of God" which elevates a person above mere material existence.[35] Behind Tatian's thinking lie the Genesis creation accounts, in which the human is first created "according to the image and likeness" of God (Gen 1:27), and then is said to have been formed of the dust of the earth and enlivened by God's breath to become a "living soul" Gen 2:6). In other words, each person has a material body and a soul, and then something more, the "image of God," which conveys immortality. Elsewhere he will describe this "image and likeness of God" as God, through the Spirit, taking up residence in otherwise mortal human beings.[36] The influence of Middle Platonism, with its tripartite anthropology, is quite palpable here.[37]

32. *Or ad Graec* 41.1.

33. *Or ad Graec* 5.1–2. Note the currency of this idea among the Middle Platonists.

34. *Or ad Graec* 7.1.

35. *Or ad Graec* 12.1.

36. *Or ad Graec* 15.1–2.

37. See esp. Plutarch, *Mor* 943A. The idea is rooted in the *Timaeus* 30A–B. The influence of Middle Platonism on Tatian is extensive; see Martin Elze, *Tatian und seine Theologie* (Forschungen zur Kirken- und Dogmengeschichte; Göttingen: Vandenhoeck & Ruprecht, 1960) 27–33; also Drijvers, "Early Syriac Christianity," 173.

Tatian understands sin and salvation within this scheme as well. The soul by itself is not immortal. And yet, it can become immortal, with the help of God's Spirit. Originally, says Tatian, the Spirit was the soul's constant companion. But when the soul refused to follow it, the Spirit gave it up for lost. If the soul wanders thus in ignorance of God, when the body dies, the soul will die with it. But souls that are obedient to Wisdom will once again draw to themselves the Spirit, and with the help of the Spirit, they will ascend to the realms above, where the Spirit finds its home.[38] In this way, Tatian understands the soul as the human capacity for free will and choice. By choosing Wisdom, the soul gains knowledge of God and immortality. But the soul that turns away, and rejects "the servant of the suffering God"[39] becomes an enemy of God and will be punished at the resurrection of the dead.[40]

Tatian's religious vision included an element of world renunciation, but there is little sign of the extreme encratite theology often attributed to him.[41] He simply advocates a certain attitude of detachment from common pursuits and concerns that arise out of the vicissitudes of life: "If I am a slave, I put up with slavery; if a free man, I do not boast of my good birth. I see that the sun is the same for everybody, and through pleasure and want there is one death for everybody . . . Even the richest die."[42] The form of community he advocated seems to have been remarkably egalitarian. He boasts of his practice of teaching both men and women, young and old, poor and wealthy,[43] and he upbraids the Greeks for honoring various women with statuary, while "jeering at the women who philosophize among us," and refusing to admit that there might be "wise women" in his community of learning that comprises "women and boys and girls."[44] Thus, his world-renunci-

---

38. *Or ad Graec* 13.
39. Perhaps an oblique reference to Jesus.
40. *Or ad Graec* 13.
41. See, e.g., Eusebius, *Hist eccles* 4.30.2–7; Jerome, *Lives* 29.
42. *Or ad Graec* 11.1.
43. *Or ad Graec* 32.
44. *Or ad Graec* 33.

ation is of a sort not unlike that attributed to Jesus in the synoptic tradition: he is a cultural dissident, but not necessarily an ascetic. It is a dissidence that fits well the dualistic mytheme of a self divided into parts mortal and immortal, where the goal of life is to transcend mortal existence and attain immortality by ascending to the spiritual realm.

Bardaisan

Many of these ideas seem to have been shared also by the enigmatic Syrian intellectual, Bardaisan, who flourished in the court of Abgar VIII in the latter part of the second century (154–222 CE), and passed at least part of his life there as a Christian.[45] Of the many works authored by Bardaisan, apparently none survive.[46] Thus, our incomplete knowledge of his views rests for the most part on second-hand, and often hostile accounts (e.g., in Ephraem of Syria[47]), and the so-called *Book of the Laws of the Countries*,[48] in which a student of Bardaisan lays out his ideas on fate and free will

45. See H. J. W. Drijvers, *Bardaisan of Edessa* (Studia Semitica Neerlandica 6; Assen: Van Gorcum, 1966); idem, "Bardesanes," in *TRE* 5:206–12.

46. Ephraem mentions a *Book of Mysteries* and a work *Concerning Domnus* (*CH* 1.14; *CH* 56.9), one hundred and fifty hymns he is said to have written (*CH* 53.6), and several books on astrology that were current among his followers (*CH* 1.18). Eusebius (*Hist eccles* 4.30.1) and Hippolytus (*Haer* 6.35; 7.31) mention a *Dialogue Against the Marcionites*. The 10th century chronicler Ibn al-Nadim refers to three works, *Concerning Light and Darkness, On Spiritual Reality and Truth,* and *Concerning the Moveable and the Immovable* (Drijvers, "Bardesanes," 207).

47. In his *Hymnen contra haereses*; see E. Beck, ed. and trans., *Des heiligen Ephraem des Syrers Hymnen conta Haereses* (CSCO, Scr. Syr., 76–77; Louvain: Peeters, 1957).

48. W. Cureton, ed., *Specilegium Syriacum, containing remains of Bardesan, Meliton, Ambrose and Mara bar Serapion* (London: Rivingtons, 1855); H. J. W. Drijvers, ed. and trans., *The Book of the Laws of Countries. Dialogue on Fate of Bardaisan of Edessa* (Semitic Texts with Translations III; Assen: Van Gorcum, 1965). Eusebius may refer to this work as *The Dialogue Concerning Fate* (*Hist eccles* 4, 30, 2), which would be a more descriptive and appropriate title.

in the form of a dialogue between Bardaisan himself and a certain disciple, Aveida.[49]

Bardaisan's cosmology[50] was a modified form of the Platonic scheme as found in the *Timaeus*. Before the world began, there existed four basic Elements: Light, Wind, Fire, and Water (cf. Plato's Earth, Air, Fire, and Water[51]). Above them stood the Lord, below them the chaos of Darkness. According to Bardaisan's thought, the creation came about as the result of a crisis occasioned by the accidental mixing of these primal elements with the Darkness—the influence of Genesis 1:2 is evident. As the Elements mingled with the Darkness, there arose great chaos and the primordial order of the cosmos was destroyed. The Elements appealed to the Lord for help, who sent into their midst the "Word of Thought" ("First Word" in Ephraem), who began then to sort out the cosmic mess. The Word separated the Darkness from the Elements and consigned it once again to the depths below. But the Word's purifying work could not yet be carried to completion, and a small part of the Darkness remained intermingled with the Elements. From these Darkness-tinged elements, then, the Word created the world, including human beings. Over the course of time, the Word continues to purify the Elements of their remaining Darkness through the processes of birth and regeneration, until the Darkness is completely purged and the cosmic order restored.

In the *Book of the Laws of the Countries* Bardaisan offers a glimpse of the anthropology that accompanied this myth. The subject of his dialogue with Aveida is Fate, and whether a human

49. Several problems attend this work, including whether the dialogue is that mentioned and attributed to Bardaisan by Eusebius (*Hist eccles* 4, 30, 2; *Praep evang* 4, 9, 32) and Epiphanius (*Panarion,* 56) is this dialogue, or based upon it, and consequently, the extent to which it reflects accurately the views of Bardaisan. For discussion, see Drijvers, *The Book of the Laws*, xx–xx.

50. Bardaisan's cosmology is to be reconstructed, with difficulty, from the *Book of the Laws*, four other major sources (Barhadbesabba ʿArabia, Moses bar Kepha, Iwannis of Dàra, and Theodore bar Khonai), and other minor ones. The present work follows Drijvers' analysis in *Bardaisan of Edessa*, 96–126 and 218–25.

51. *Tim* 32C.

being is bound by all that is fore-ordained, or contrariwise, may choose to do good or evil. For Bardaisan, as with Tatian, it is the latter. The reason for this claim rests in the Jewish account of creation, which Bardaisan apparently grafted onto the myth of the four Elements and the Word of Thought. Other created things exist only as instruments to serve the wisdom of God, he says, but not so with human beings. The Word created humans in the "image of Elohim,"[52] and so they do not serve, but are served. Moreover, because of this, a human being is uniquely guided by his/her own will, "so that whatever he is able to do, if he will he may do it, and if he do not will he may not do it, that so he may justify himself or condemn."[53] Thus, like Tatian, Bardaisan seems to have been influenced by the Hellenistic Jewish theological tradition that placed great store in Gen 1:27 as the key to understanding humanity's uniquely moral relationship to God. Humans are free to exercise moral agency because they are created *in God's image.* Elsewhere in the *Book of the Laws* Bardaisan states the matter thus:

> While in matters pertaining to their bodies they preserve their nature like animals, in matters pertaining to their minds they do that which they choose, as children of the free, and endowed with power, and as made in the likeness of God.[54]

Like Tatian, Bardaisan seems also to have subscribed to the tripartite anthropology that Philo and other Hellenistic Jews derived from reading the Genesis creation accounts in light of Platonic philosophy. Referring, again, to the question of how Fate might exercise influence over a person, Bardaisan describes a process whereby the three parts that make up a human being come together in a kind of descent into complete human existence. Fate is a kind of order, he insists, and

52. *Laws* (*ANF* VIII: 724). The Syriac text quotes directly from the Hebrew of Gen 1:27 using Syriac characters (note in ANF VIII:724).

53. *Laws* (*ANF* VIII: 724).

54. *Laws* (*ANF* VIII: 727).

in conformity with this said procession and order, intelligences undergo change when they descend to be with the soul, and souls undergo change when they descend to be with bodies, and this order, under the name of Fate and nativity, is the agent of the changes that take place in this assemblage of parts of which a human being consists.[55]

How does Jesus function in Bardaisan's thought? As with others who embraced the Platonic mind/body dualism, Bardaisan would have thought of the body as transient, subject to dissolution at death, while the mind (or soul) carried on, ultimately to return to the divine place from whence it had come.[56] But this return is not easily accomplished. Again, Jewish ideas about creation come into play. For Bardaisan, it is Adam's sin and death that become the mythic impediment to the soul's ability to cross back over into the divine realm. It falls to Jesus, the Lord, to overcome the sin of Adam, and thus lead the souls of the righteous back across to the Kingdom. Ephraem explains:

> According to the doctrine of Bardaisan—the Death that Adam brought in—was a hindrance to Souls—in that they were hindered at the Crossing place—because the sin of Adam hindered them—"and the Life," he says, "that our Lord brought in—is that he taught verity and ascended—and brought them across into the Kingdom."
> "Therefore," he says, our Lord taught us—that "every one that keepeth My Word—death forever he shall not taste"—that his Soul is not hindered—when it crosses at the Crossing-place—like the hindrance of old—wherewith the Souls were hindered—before our Savior had come.[57]

Jesus saves those who "keep his Word." By teaching them truth, and showing them the way to ascend, he brings them to the

55. *Laws* (*ANF* VIII, 729).

56. *Pr. Ref.* II, p. LXVI (trans.), p. 143 (text), cited after Drijvers, *Bardaisan of Edessa*, 153–54.

57. *Pr. Ref.* II, p. LXXVII (trans.), pp. 164–165 (text), cited after Drijvers, *Bardaisan of Edessa*, p. 155.

"Bridal chamber of Light," that is, the paradise from whence they have come.[58]

Bardaisan's ethics are not obvious from the extant sources. He was apparently active in the court of Abgar VIII, and presumably led the life of those with access to the king's inner circle.[59] Thus, while Bardaisan would have cultivated a certain attentiveness to Jesus' teachings as a way of nurturing the mind (or soul) and preventing the excesses of the body-driven life, one could not describe him as an ascetic. He apparently did not withdraw from normal life, but lived out his religious principles in a conventional setting in which he was at home, and fairly successful.

The Acts of Thomas

The notion that Syrian Christianity was especially ascetical comes primarily from the *Acts of Thomas*, a close relative of the *Gospel of Thomas*,[60] but a century or more removed from the origins of the Syrian Christian community.[61] In the *Acts*, the cultural dissidence seen in earlier texts is raised to the level of apostolic ideal, with self-control and world renunciation as the center of the life of true discipleship.[62] This ideal also includes one's manner of dress and one's diet. Of Judas Thomas it is said, for example, that, "he fasts much and prays much, and eats bread and salt and drinks water,

58. *Pr. Ref.* II, p. LXXVII (trans.), 164 (text), cited after Drijvers, *Bardaisan of Edessa*, 155.

59. The inference derives from the report of Julius Africanus, who accompanied Septimus Severus to Edessa in 195 CE, and there met Bardaisan in the court of Abgar VIII. He notes especially Bardaisan's remarkable skill as an archer. See Migne, *PG* X, 45; critical discussion of the text: A. Hilgenfeld, *Bardesanes, der letzte Gnostiker* (Leipzig: Weigel, 1864), 14 n6.

60. The relationship between the two texts was noticed first by H.-Ch. Puech ("The Gospel of Thomas," in Hennecke-Schneemelcher, *NTA1* I: 286–87; further, see Attridge, "Intertextuality in the Acts of Thomas," 110–13).

61. The *Acts of Thomas* are generally dated to the beginning of the third century; see J. N. Bremmer, "The Acts of Thomas: Date, Place, and Women," in Bremmer, ed., *The Apocryphal Acts of Thomas* (Leuven: Brill, 2001), 74–90.

62. E.g., *Acts Thom* 12; 28; 61; 83–84, etc.

and wears only one garment, and takes nothing from anyone for himself, and whatever he has he gives to others"[63] This mendicant lifestyle is offered to "men and women, boys and girls, young men and young women, young and old, whether you are slaves or free."[64] This life of world-renunciation is combined with a kind of apostolic mission focused on the poor. Judas, it is said, "was going about in the villages and cities, and was ministering to the poor, and was making the afflicted comfortable."[65] He is "the nourisher of the orphans and the provider of the widows."[66]

The goal of this life of world-renunciation and service to the poor is salvation in a heavenly afterlife. For example, in the Second Act,[67] when King Gudaphorus discovers that Judas has taken all the money given him to build a new palace and spent it on the poor and afflicted, he is initially incensed. But he soon discovers that the palace Judas has been building him is not of this earth, but exists in heaven. He is thus converted and listens rapt as Judas preaches the virtues of world renunciation: "Look upon the ravens and consider the fowl of heaven which sow not nor reap, and God feeds them; how much more then will he care for you, you lacking in faith." And "repent and believe in the new preaching and receive the pleasant yoke and the light burden, and live and die not . . . Come out from the darkness, that the light may receive you."[68]

Presupposed in the *Acts* is an anthropology not unlike that of Tatian and Bardaisan, and there are again glimpses of Hellenistic Jewish Wisdom theology. The person is presumed to consist of a body and a soul,[69] or occasionally a body, a soul, and a spirit.[70] At death, the body is dissolved,[71] but the soul survives to receive

63. *Acts Thom* 20.

64. *Acts Thom* 28.

65. *Acts Thom* 19.

66. *Acts Thom* 19.

67. *Acts Thom* 17ff.

68. *Acts Thom* 28.

69. *Acts Thom* 22–23; 28; 30; 39; 42; 53; 67; 95; 152; 158.

70. *Acts Thom* 94.

71. *Acts Thom* 95; or alternatively, something from which to be set free

eternal rest at the resurrection[72] or to sink into punishment for deeds done in life.[73] It all depends on one's decisions—to remain mired in the world and its temptations, or to listen to Jesus in the voice of the apostle, and to "walk in all humility and temperance and purity, and hope in God," and "become servants of him."[74]

The fate of the soul is depicted metaphorically in the *Acts* in the remarkable poem commonly known as the "Hymn of the Pearl" (chs. 108–13). The origin of this hymn or poem is not known, but it may well pre-date the *Acts*,[75] and thus belong to the legacy of early Christianity in Syria as it mingled with the many cultural streams that flowed through the crossroads of Edessa in the second century. The "Hymn of the Pearl" is an allegory for the descent and ascent of the soul. In it a young prince undertakes a journey from his home in the east, "down into Egypt" in search of a pearl guarded by a menacing serpent. But while he is there, he forgets himself and becomes enmeshed in the corrupting life of Egypt. He forgets about the pearl and his mission and falls into a deep sleep. His parents, though, learn of his plight and send him a letter, which reawakens him, reminds him of who he is and of his mission, and beckons him home. Thus he is redeemed. He soon subdues the serpent, takes the pearl and begins his ascent out of Egypt, back to the land of his father and mother, led all the while by the letter. En route he is met by emissaries from his parents, who bring with them the son's royal robe, adorned with glorious colors and studded with gems, and embroidered upon it the "image of the king of kings." The robe is "like a mirror of myself," he says, for "though we were two in distinction and yet again one in likeness." He puts on the robe and comes once again to the home of his father, where he mingles with his princes and prepares to proceed to the gate of the king of kings, that "with [his] offering and [his] pearl" he should present himself to the king.

(*Acts Thom* 160; 166; 30). It is described as "alien" (*Acts Thom* 39).

72. *Acts Thom* 80.

73. *Acts Thom* 55–57.

74. *Acts Thom* 58.

75. For discussion, see Layton, *The Gnostic Scriptures*, 367–69.

The background for this story is, again, the Platonic belief, widespread in the Hellenistic world, that the human soul has it origins in the heavenly, spiritual realm, from whence it descends to become incarnate in a body. This involvement of the soul in the physical realm is problematic insofar as it can hinder, or even blot out, the soul's cognizance of the divine realm from which it has come. The soul can become lost, weighed down, lulled to sleep, intoxicated, and thus lose touch with its true nature, source and destiny. The antidote is contemplation leading to genuine wisdom, or self-knowledge that can rekindle one's memory of the transcendent realm from which the soul has come, and thus make possible its return. Elements of this mythos can be seen reflected throughout the *Acts*, but also in the other texts of early Syrian Christianity, including the *Gospel of Thomas*.

Christianity in eastern Syria might thus be described as a distinctive form of Hellenistic Jewish Wisdom theology, in which Jesus plays a role (though sometimes surprisingly limited) as guide, sage, revealer, or sometimes the role of Wisdom herself. The concern of Edessene Christians was the nature and identity of the true self. In answering this question, they borrowed heavily from Middle Platonic ideas about the tripartite nature of the self—body, soul, mind (or spirit). Their goal was salvation, understood as the soul's (or spirit's) return to the heavenly realm from whence it had come, the place of life and light, where souls find their rest in God. The means by which one might reach this goal was world renunciation, presented in terms reflecting sometimes more, sometimes less, ascetical rigor, together with deep self-reflection on one's true nature and destiny. The world was thought to be a place of fallenness, of corruption and imperfection, where one might easily be swept along, forgetful of one's true nature and destiny in God. This, however, is not due to any inherent flaw in the cosmos—it was not created by a rebellious demiurge, for example. The flaw lies in human folly, expressed as devotion to corporeal existence and neglect of the transcendent. These followers of Jesus believed that he had called them to wake up, to realize who they really are, and to leave behind this world which they have learned to despise.

One demonstrates this wakefulness or enlightenment by eschewing worldly values, and devoting oneself to those whom the world has despised: the poor, the widow, the orphan. It was a calling they understood to belong to both men and women, young or old, slave or free. It was possible, they believed, for anyone to take up the life of Jesus and to embody his peculiar form of counter-cultural wisdom.

In addition to these features of Syrian Christianity as it developed East of the Euphrates, one might also take cognizance of several features, well known from the New Testament and other early Christian texts originating further to the West, that are conspicuous by their absence. For example, stories of Jesus' suffering, death and resurrection play virtually no role in these texts from Eastern Syria. Neither does one find talk here of an atonement made for sin. Also notable by its relative absence is the concept of faith, so ubiquitous in the West. Finally, there is little of the anti-Jewish rhetoric that plays such a critical role especially in Matthew and John, but to a lesser extent in all of the canonical gospels and in Paul. How might one account for these differences?

It must be remembered that the Euphrates marked an important boundary during most of this period: the Eastern frontier of the Roman Empire. True, Trajan had crossed the river in 116, but his successors had little interest in holding the new territory, and it was nearly a century later when Caraculla finally annexed the region as a Roman colony. Thus, throughout the period of Christian origins, west of the Euphrates was Roman territory; east of the Euphrates was not. Moreover, during this period, the region west of the Euphrates was far from calm. All four canonical gospels were written during or in the immediate aftermath of one of the bloodiest episodes in the history of the Middle East, the Jewish War. Moreover, both before and after the war, Christians throughout the Empire had to reckon with the experience of being dissidents under a totalitarian regime. They had to constantly remember that Jesus died on a Roman cross and that martyrdom was always a possibility for them as well. The extent to which these experiences led Christians in the West to reflect on the significance of Jesus' death, and the phenomenon of martyrdom as a way both of understanding his death, but also their own periodic suffering, has probably not been fully appreciated. Further, that such experiences could draw the concept of faith, or loyalty, into the center of Christian reflection is rather obvious. Christians do not normally think of such things as related to particular historical realities because they seem so central, and thus self-evident to Christian faith. But east of the Euphrates one discovers a Christianity in which they are not so central after all. Why?

It may well be that their relative absence in these texts from Eastern Syria is to be accounted for by the fact that the peculiar experiences of Christians living in the Roman Empire were not the sort of experiences that Christians faced east of the Euphrates, where Rome did not hold sway. There was no great war in the East, in which Jews had to struggle for survival against a totalitarian empire. Rather, the Jews who lived in Edessa, Nisibis, and other cities of the East formed an integral part of the overall cityscape, prospering along with others of various ethnic origins in the vigorous economy that flourished along the caravan routes. When Jews who followed Jesus came to Edessa, they likely settled in among other Jews living there, and thus also lived in relative peace with their neighbors. Thus, death and martyrdom were not their issues. Faithfulness in the face of danger and threat was a lesser concern. And there, without the catastrophe of the Jewish War and other political developments that would ultimately drive a wedge between Jews and Christians, there did not develop the animosity that expresses itself on the Christian side in the West as intense anti-Judaism. East of the Euphrates, Christians probably remained comfortably folded into the Jewish communities in which they settled for several generations to come. That is why in the East, it is scarcely possible to identify these Christian texts as Christian, and not Jewish.

Epilogue
Marvin Meyer, Angel of Magic and Mischief

———————— *Willis Barnstone* ————————

When I left Guillaume, the heat and light of day immediately fell
away. As soon as I spotted him I went to him and, stronger than me, I
ran, I laughed. Suddenly, life was beautiful.

Guillaume was continuously inspired.

—ANDRÉ BILLY ON GUILLAUME APOLLINAIRE (1880–1918)

Each time I call this strange unique angel of the earth,
I encounter a man living on the first morning of creation.
He answers softly: *This is Marv Meyer speaking,*

I think it a recording till I say Marv! and Marv shouts WILLIS!
He's discovered a Gnostic fragment in a Cairo church,
And no ululating call in the Sahara will shut him up.

This gentleman from all continents I've been working with
For only two decades; we collaborate on translation
From leather-bound Coptic scrolls, on espionage,

On radical punctuation, on flouting industry, on dream.
At a supper with our Boston publisher, we scream ideas,
Our editor is alarmed. We say we're discussing cloud formations.

Angels are not monolingual like those builders at Babel.
Marv learns them as a kid playing marbles. For more obscure tongues
He fixes the grammar. You can't resist him. He is Dorothy

In *The Wizard of Oz*, hopping and laughing to Paradise
In total elation. We do fight and we're good at that.
We remake each other and keep our profound awareness.

How is the mountain trekker's health? At a Bible conference
In New Orleans, after a wild jazz club evening,
Back in our shared room Marv does five one-arm pushups.

The sun also riseth and the sun goeth down.
The sun is warmth, is health. Sun is also the killer sword.
All rivers run to the sea, yet the sea is not full.

In our version of the radiant Gospel of Thomas,
Yeshua, like Yoheleth, wonders before nature's secrets:
Whoever discovers what these sayings mean

Will not touch death. Koheleth murmurs:
I gave my heart to know wisdom, and to know madness and folly.
Fools walk in darkness, the wise in light, but light is fierce.

Drop Meyer on Argentine pampas and he will swim in snow
Until he reaches the Fayuum. The man of light treks on stars
And around our small globe until death stands in the road,

But Marv suffers no nonsense. He is a great scholar
And makes no mistakes. His habit is the leader's role,
Taking the heat. He transcends. When the raven calls *Hello*,

Marv knows the script. He loves a mountain night walk,
Bouncing his baritone soul off the new moon. Go out
Into the starry firmament. Listen. Hear Marvin croon.

What is smiling Marv's take on pulpit promise and magic?
Beware of slush. Now I live in the dark night. Don't fret,
You'll get over it. I have friends and words out there,

Though please remember that in the spring of my work,
With books to write for you, nature robs me of breath.
I have so much to say! Work so nature won't kill us so young.

Now I am dead only in body. Neither the mindless sun,
Nor the romantic moon that also fails to raise me
Can shush me. Look for me. I'm here. Listen. No tears.